THE
ANATOMY
OF A
GREAT
EXECUTIVE

THE
ANATOMY
OF A
GREAT
EXECUTIVE

John Wareham

HarperBusiness
A Division of HarperCollinsPublishers

•

Edward Burlingame Books
An Imprint of HarperCollinsPublishers

Library of Congress Cataloging-in-Publication Data

Wareham, John.
   The anatomy of a great executive / John Wareham.
      p.   cm.
   ISBN 0–88730–505–9
      1. Executive ability. 2. Executives—Psychology 3. Executives—
Selection and appointment. I. Title.
HD38.2.W369   1991
658.4'09—dc20   91–7999
                                                                    CIP

Illustrations by Jonathan Poore
Design by Ruth Kolbert

Printed in the United States of America

91 92 93 94 CC/HC 7 6 5 4 3 2 1

CONTENTS

ACKNOWLEDGMENTS

I have been working on these ideas for many years. I got into the business of recruiting and evaluating executives back in 1964. I soon learned the necessity of proceeding from a sound intellectual base, in which respect I was fortunate in meeting the illustrious Chicago psychologist, Dr. Robert N. McMurry, in 1967. In 1977, I appointed Doc the United States chairman of my firm, and he held this largely advisory role until his death in 1984.

As far as I'm aware Doc was the first person to use and validate the clinical interview as a means of evaluating executives (see Validating the Patterned Interview, *Personnel,* Volume 23, Number 4, American Management Association). I was fortunate in being able to use Doc's work as a launching pad for my own work. I used many of his ideas in the initial set-up of a computer model. Over the next two decades I supplemented his approach with other psychological instruments (most notably the Incomplete Sentence Blank), thereby building a rich database of information—of which this book is a by-product. I might also mention that since my firm usually enjoys long-term relationships with our clients, we have been able to run follow up checks, comparing the validity of our predictions of how an executive will perform in a new role, against subsequently observed behaviors. These studies naturally permitted us to further enhance our whole system. Nothing is ever perfect, of course, but, in most cases we can now help a sophisticated client to reduce errors of hiring and promotion by better than eighty-five percent—which we think is pretty darned good.

The organizing principle of this book, including the

drawings of the funny man, came to me on a transatlantic flight to New York. I tried them out on my colleague Anna-Louise Mole, and my wife, both of whom proffered much encouragement. Dr. Donovan Greene, the eminent Los Angeles business psychologist—who also worked with Doc, running his West Coast office—focused me on the special usefulness of examining the kinds of specific behaviors that I've included in the behavioral checklists you'll find in following pages.

I should also like to thank my colleagues at Wareham Associates, some of whom—Sir Arthur Harper, Tom Jackson, and Gabrielle Ruthven—have since passed to the Great Recruiter.

Tom Morgan, Evan Whitton, and Ken Bowden each played a key role in pushing me—and helping me—to concentrate on writing—and rewriting this book! Virginia Smith has been a very enthusiastic, thoughtful, and sensitive editor. Jonathan Ewing also spotted some nuances that others might well have missed.

For contributions through the years I must especially thank Torquil MacLeod, Wayne Parkes, Philip Lock, and Colin Evans, as well as, Peter Bowring, Grant Pryde, Anthony Wareham, Dan Wheeler, Joey Roberts—and the many people who have supported, and continued to support all of their efforts. I would also like to thank my clients for entrusting me with the role of evaluating their potential appointees. Finally, I must mention all the wonderful executive candidates who have passed through my firm's offices, for without you there would be no book, and my firm would have had no reason for being—so, many thanks.

In the end, however, I am responsible for putting this volume together, so I hope you'll find my effort helpful and enjoy reading it.

JOHN WAREHAM

THE
ANATOMY
OF A
GREAT
EXECUTIVE

PART ONE

THE

ANATOMY

OF A

GREAT

EXECUTIVE

∞◊∞

*I profess both to learn and teach
anatomy, not from books but from
dissections; not from positions of
philosophers but from the fibre
of nature.*

WILLIAM HARVEY
1578–1657

1

WHY
YOU CAN'T SPOT
GOOD EXECUTIVES
RIGHT NOW

The
Four Crucial Blind Spots
That Lead to Ruinous
Mis-hires
and Mispromotions

∝◇∝

Nothing can move a man who is paid by the hour;
how sweet the flight of time seems to his calm mind.

CHARLES DUDLEY WARNER

THE CONFESSIONS
OF A FAILED FOUNDER

In 1964, soon after I'd opened my human resources practice, a silver-haired chief executive whom I'd greatly admired phoned to confide that the large company he'd founded had just gone broke.

I was surprised, saddened, and curious. "If you had it all to do over again, would you do anything differently?" I asked. He paused, then answered slowly:

"I'd pay much more attention to all my key hires and promotions. I brought in a tremendous amount of business, and I relied on my staff to do the work. But I hired badly, and promoted too many 'empty suits.' Then, suddenly, it was all too late . . ."

They say we only pay attention to the things that we discover for ourselves, and I guess this has to be so. For, still today, I continue to be amazed at how many senior executives fail fully to realize the potentially ruinous cost of a mis-hire or mispromotion. Consider:

- Recruiting a $150,000 executive who fails after six months costs infinitely more than merely $75,000 of wasted salary. Add back all expenses, including the value of your own time, lost momentum, the effect on the morale of your team—and clients—and you're usually looking at a *very* sizable six-figure loss.
- Even worse is to pay good money to wind up hiring a person who looks very good, but in fact turns out to be *not really good enough to keep, but not quite bad enough to fire, either*. Once employed, such mediocrities can often hang on for many years—at a true cost running into *many millions of dollars*.

5

THE CHIEF WHO WAS
DESTINED FOR NASTY SURPRISES

The fault, dear Brutus, is not in the stars,
But in ourselves, that we are underlings.
SHAKESPEARE, *JULIUS CAESAR*

An old saying has it that "every man complains about his memory but no man complains about his judgment." This is nowhere more true than when it comes to sizing up executives, where even the sophisticated executives tend vastly to overrate the ability to reach valid conclusions about a candidate. Consider, for example:

A potential client who had prospered during some boom years discovered in the downturn that many key executives seemed incompetent. He called me in. "How do you go about screening new hires?" I asked.

"Well, I look at the résumé, and bring likely candidates in for a personal interview, during which I find out the date of their birth. Then, when they've left the room, I look them up in my astrology book of *Linda Goodman's Star Signs.* You'd be amazed how accurate she can be!"

"I see. But I thought you had to know the precise moment of birth for astrology to be effective."

"Ideally, but not necessarily. If a person doesn't fit Linda's first profile, then they were probably born on the cusp, so I turn to two more profiles, the ones immediately preceding and following. I keep doing this till I find the one that fits."

This was not Nancy Reagan speaking. This was a savvy, successful businessman—with a major blind spot. You might feel that *you're* much to smart to rely upon false prophets or shaky practices. Maybe, maybe not. Consider another example.

THE BOARD MEMBER
WITH "INSIDE KNOWLEDGE"

In the course of a search to find a chief executive for a major world shipping line, a board member recommended Upton Toffnoe's appointment, and it fell to me to size up the candidate and give the Good Housekeeping sign of approval.

Just before my interview with Upton, the board member called to proffer some background: "I can't begin to say how fortunate we are that Upton heard of our search and said he would take the job. He has excellent academic credentials, wonderful experience, and great connections. He comes from a fine family that I've known very well for many years. His father is still a client, and his older brother was a big success on Wall Street. Upton is in the same mold, and still very ambitious. He *looks* like a leader, too. He's tall and charismatic. People will look up to him. He's someone I can personally vouch for having the 'Right Stuff.' "

We finished the conversation, and my secretary ushered Upton into my office. He was fifty-five, silver-haired, tall, imposing, and gravel-voiced. He wore an elegant tailored suit that made light of his corpulent leanings. He had a master's degree in business and a doctorate in economics. He'd enjoyed a long career with another major shipper, rising to senior vice president responsible for operations and safety, before leaving just two years ago to head up a much smaller venture. He did indeed hail from an illustrious family, a responsibility he apparently took seriously, serving on the boards of various prestigious charities.

The interview went well. Upton answered my questions fairly directly and explained his most recent decision to go with a much smaller firm, even though this entailed a drop in income. "I quit, as you might imagine, to take up the challenge of being chief executive running my own show. Unfortunately, the company was seriously undercapitalized, and I'm not sure they can make a go of it," he said.

Toward the close of the interview I asked Upton a standard due diligence question: "Do you drink?"

"Ahh . . . *Socially!*"

Something in the pause and the emphasis led me to follow up. "What would that be for you, I wonder?"

"Well, in my job, I have to entertain a lot of clients, so it's hard to dodge a regular three-martini lunch syndrome."

"I can imagine; and in the evening . . . ?"

"Well, after I get home, I like to take a cocktail to get the buzz back."

"Yes of course. To get the buzz back."

"And my wife and I enjoy a nice bottle of wine with our evening meal."

"Of course! A day without wine is like a day without sunshine! And . . . ?"

"Well, we keep a bottle of whiskey and a couple of glasses next to the bed, and usually just have a nightcap before going to sleep."

"A nightcap? *Of course.* And that's about it?"

"Yeah . . ." He didn't sound quite sure. I looked at him expectantly.

"Yeah, that's about it. Except when the pressure comes on. *Then* I'm inclined to drink a little heavily!"

Upton Toffnoe's whole job history now made very good sense. He was an indulged child, who had failed to live up to the high standards set by his father and elder brother. His family name and connections had landed him a good job and some prestigious side interests, but, nonetheless, he'd arrived in his fifties with the self-image of a loser and a drinking habit to match. His former firm was slow to appreciate his problem, or at least to act on it, but—and this piece of information came to light much later—following the revelation of shocking safety problems, they'd squeezed Upton out of his job and kept everything very hush-hush, for fear of being sued for appointing a person with such problems to so sensitive a role.

From the very first, Upton had floundered in his new role as chief executive. Now, with the company near to going under, which seemed to stem directly from the absence of a sober chief executive, he needed to get out.

Still driven to prove his identity as a person, but lacking in self-insight and compelled to deny his addiction to alcohol, Upton continued to aspire to roles beyond his capabilities. In many ways it might have been difficult to identify a worse candidate.

You might wonder why Upton cared to relate his predilection for a drink in such detail—especially as he'd been able to hide his addiction from so many other people. Well, we're getting ahead of ourselves here, and we'll discuss this question in more detail later. The quick answer, however, lies in the fact that I established myself as a sympathetic listener, and *asked the question!*

What really makes this story worth telling, I think, is that Upton came highly recommended by a smart, savvy person who thought he knew Upton fairly well. How could *he* have been so naive? Frankly, I was not much surprised, for the decision to hire or promote an executive is so apparently simple—yet so deceptively complex—that, more often than not, the typical hirer puts the saddle on the wrong horse. Hirers do this because they suffer from four crucial blind spots:

1. *They proceed from the wrong assumptions about human behavior.* They typically work from seat-of-the-pants fallacies founded on little more than hunches and homilies.
2. *They have no realistic intellectual model by which to size up the subject.* They overvalue the wrong things, and entirely overlook the key qualities.
3. *They don't know what questions to ask.* They focus on silly things, or restrict themselves to superficialities.
4. Thus, even if by accident the hirer asks the right question, he or she remains *incompetent to interpret the answer proffered.*

Now, before *you* back a loser, let's set to and immediately address these blind spots.

2

THE THINGS
YOU KNOW
THAT AIN'T SO

*The
Seven Fallacies
That Account
for 80 Percent of People
Misjudgments*

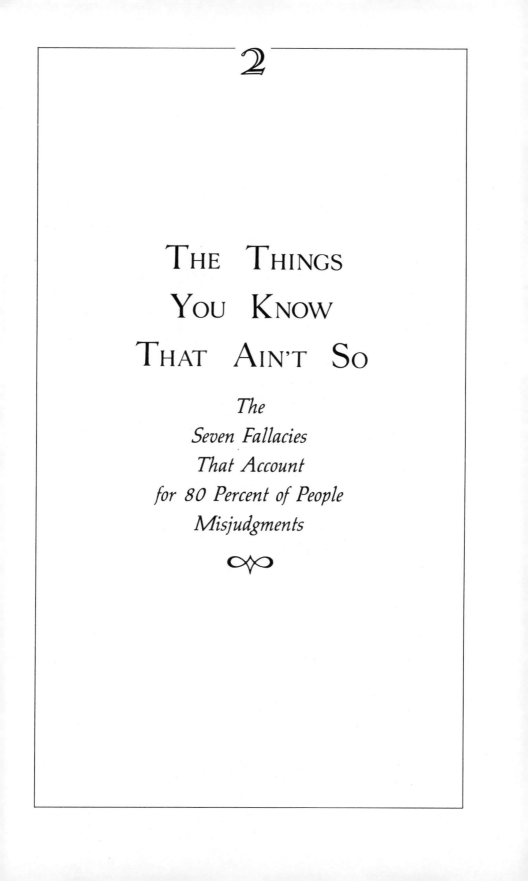

#1: THE FALLACY
OF INSTANT INSIGHT

*"I can tell how competent a person is
just about as soon as I meet him."*

"I've hired this new fellow, John. He's been with
me for six months now, and things aren't working
out. Could you come over and take a peek at him for
me?"

"Take a *peek* at him? I'd need to do more than
that. How did you come to hire him?"

"I met him on the golf course. We were paired
together in a midweek tournament. He was between
jobs at the time. He played a great game, and we
won the afternoon championship. Then in the clubhouse he was like a breath of fresh air. We had a few
drinks and got on famously. I said to myself, Good
executives are hard to find, so don't miss out on this
fellow by fooling around with a lot of forms and
interviews and all that. Snap him up immediately."

True to his hunches, my client snapped the fellow up
right then and there—and had to fire within the year! If the
hasty hirer had only paused to ask himself a few simple
questions, he might not have fallen into this costly and
embarrassing trap:

- Does being on the golf course at midweek signify any
  particular commitment to the work ethic? Or might it
  more likely indicate a measure of irresponsibility? The
  answer will differ from person to person, of course. Just
  the same, best to be alert to the possibilities.

- Can business competence be assumed from the ability to play a good game of golf? Or is it, like adroitness in the game of billiards, the sign of a misspent youth?
- Does being a good fellow over a few drinks at the clubhouse signify a general ability to get on with people at work? Or might a great deal of charm actually indicate personality problems?

Answers to these questions were never explored, of course. My client, like so many executives, mistakenly believed that a person's competence may readily be inferred from appearance and presentation, voice and manner, and social habits.

In fact, although some qualities may be assumed from a person's presentation, it is highly unwise to rely upon surface impressions, because

- Individuals who make excellent impressions are often hucksters who have devoted much time and talent toward putting the best foot forward.
- A really sound, mature person is unlikely to suffer any deep need to sell his or her personality and, in consequence, may sometimes seem a touch "offhand."
- Many outstanding people often do not present as well as more conformist "organization" men and women.
- Social knowledge of a person, even over a long period of time, is often an unreliable basis for predicting what a person is "really" like, or how he or she will perform in a work situation.
- There are some very sound reasons—discussed later— why, as a matter of routine, many people are highly likely to be the *opposite* of what they seem.

In fact, sizing up an executive calls for a truly informed understanding of how people behave, a lot of information about the subject, and an experience base in using such understanding and information. People who go by appearances may occasionally make some lucky appointments. On balance, however, they're far more likely to

- Reject good people on the basis of prejudice.
- Appoint people who look great—like Wayne-type film stars, even—but who turn out to be incompetent.
- Fall prey to—and hire—some very charming rascals.
- Hire or promote people who look just like them! (Recruiting in one's own image.)

#2: THE FALLACY OF THE MANY EYES

"We minimize personnel mistakes by having several of our key people screen each candidate."

It is sometimes believed that errors of hiring or promotion may be minimized by subjecting candidates to interviews by many people, or even to group interviews, so that a consensus may be reached. The rationale is that if two heads are better than one, then many heads may result in ultimate wisdom.

How much value there is in this approach depends upon the qualification of the members of the committee; mere size means nothing, for as Emile Zola once noted, "Even if fifty million Frenchmen say a foolish thing, it is still a foolish thing."

Unless at least one of the interviewers is blessed with special insight, the whole exercise is likely to resemble the blind leading the blind, for experience reveals that the combined judgment of lay interviewers is often *worse* than the individual opinions of the members.

A further point to note here is that group interviews, "beauty contests" as they are sometimes called, heavily favor extroverted candidates, who tend to be highly adept in such encounters, winning approbation and praise for imagined personality strengths while actually diverting attention from indices of personality weakness.

#3 THE FALLACY
OF THE OKAY GAL/GUY

"I'm Okay and You're Okay."

We tend to believe that with few exceptions, most people are well adjusted. A corollary is that most people are rational, and can be relied upon to act logically.

In fact, well-adjusted, emotionally mature people are the exception rather than the rule:

> Well-documented surveys reveal that only one person in five grows into a well-adjusted emotionally mature person. The other 80 percent suffer from a wide range of emotional problems. One person in five suffers from quite chronic mental illness. One person in five is, has been, or will be incarcerated in some form of institution to be treated for emotional maladjustment.

When I recently quoted the above statistics in a seminar I ran in New Zealand, where I grew up, a member of the audience, an advertising man as I recall, decided to argue the point with me, saying, "Executives like us are mostly *very* well adjusted." I politely quoted the relevant sources to him, and let the matter drop, for I didn't want to get sidetracked. At the end of the day, however, after almost everyone had gone and I was talking to a few stragglers, this fellow strode back into the room. "Someone has stolen my coat," he said angrily. In fact, after the audience dispersed, the staff had moved the two or three remaining coats into a separate coat-check room for safekeeping. "Talk to the office staff," I said as soothingly as I could. "I think they'll be able to find it for you," which, indeed, they did. In the process of identifying it, however, they had to empty out the pockets, and they discovered that *he was packing a loaded six gun*. Nobody *ever* carries a gun in New Zealand, so the behavior was bizarre in the extreme—yet this was the same fellow who was hypersensitive to being labeled mentally ill.

Now, most of us have our little quirks, and my wife would quickly assure you that I have mine too. So, we must be tolerant of our many faults and foibles and be prepared to overlook them in friends and family. If you're considering appointing someone to a senior post in your company, however, sound common sense dictates that you bear in mind that *Homo sapiens* are creatures of emotion rather than logic, and take some little trouble to identify and contemplate these frailties before making a judgment that could cost you your financial life.

#4: THE FALLACY OF HUMAN PERFECTIBILITY

*"This executive has problems,
but I can turn her around."*

A basic premise in Western culture is that *Humankind is perfectible.* Corollaries are:

- Every person is master of his/her destiny.
- Everyone wants to improve.
- Show people their weaknesses, and they'll make every immediate effort to correct them.
- If they don't make the desired changes, improper counseling is to blame—so tell them again.

Thus, management often takes on the task of helping people attempt to cure their underlying personality problems. In fact, however, this nearly always proves to be an impossible task because:

- The urge to improve is not universal.
- Many problems are manifestations of underlying mental quirks, and cannot be superficially addressed.
- Often, the sufferer simply cannot bear to have the fault addressed, and will in all probability be compelled to deny it.

- Persisting in trying to reveal the problem may likely exacerbate it! Hence the wisdom in the adage "Do not attempt to teach a pig to sing, for it will frustrate you, and inflame the pig."

It is worth bearing in mind that countless intelligent and well-meaning people, including psychiatrists, priests, and training gurus, have devoted themselves to the task of perfecting people—but the hoped-for quick fix has yet to appear. As the Japanese say, "There is no medicine for a fool." So, the moral is, don't needlessly set out to be a reformer. Play the percentages instead.

#5: THE FALLACY OF CONTINUING SUCCESS

> *"He did it for them—so he can do even more for us."*

While this sounds like good common sense, it is actually the very nub of the Peter Principle, which you'll remember says that "managers inevitably rise to their levels of incompetence." In fact, those who rise to positions for which they are incompetent are usually promoted on the basis of their past successes. What is overlooked in considering such successes, however, is that they are often totally irrelevant to future promotion—a record of success may already have brought the subject to his "incompetence threshold," the point beyond which he will be *destined* to fail if further promoted. Bear in mind, too, that

- The Greeks recognized this assumption as a potentially tragic affliction, and called it *hubris*.
- Skill is not the same as capacity. Skill in running a small grocery store is not the same as the capacity to manage a whole chain.
- Past successes may have actually impaired the physical ability to go on performing. The spirit might be willing, but the flesh simply too weak.

- Past successes may have extinguished the underlying drive. The subject may be unable to continue to press herself to go on. She might *think* that she wants to go on, yet be unable to do so—the flesh might be willing, but the spirit weak!
- The new environment might be all wrong. Success in one kind of corporate culture might not readily transfer to another. As advertising legend Bill Bernbach noted, "I'm amused when other agencies try to hire my people away. They'd have to hire the whole environment. For a flower to blossom, you need the right soil as well as the right seed."
- The presence of a strong or creative boss may account for much of the subject's apparent successes. The superior may have nurtured the subject. Without the boss, the subject may be a loser. For example:

An important organization retained a prominent recruiter to find a new chief executive. An attractive high-profile number two from a major competitor was identified, recommended, and hired. Within the year, however, he fell apart in his new role as chief and had to be terminated. His Achilles heel lay in his inability to operate without the kind of emotional support that routinely had been available from his prior employer—*even though as number two he seldom needed to call upon it.*

#6: THE FALLACY OF THE OBJECTIVE REFEREE

> *"We take great care to get accurate telephone reference checks."*

When I advised a client not to hire a particular candidate, the chief executive was miffed.

> "I personally checked him out with his last employer, and they said he was great."
> "Who did you speak to?"
> "The founder and president."

"If the candidate was as good as he says, why did they let him leave?"

"Well, it was just one of those things."

"Which things?"

"Things not working out. You know."

I was skeptical, so I personally called the founder. I got the same story. The candidate was first rate, a paragon of executive excellence with no problems whatsoever. I pressed the question of why such a fellow would have been let go, but the answer made no sense. Finally, out of intuition, I asked one last question, framing it in the way of a statement. "You're related to this candidate, of course?" There was a long pause. "Well, not really. He's only my son-in-law."

References are suspect for at least several reasons. First, the references proffered by a candidate are always likely to be biased in his or her favor—as in the case just cited. Obtaining accurate references from past employers has also become increasingly difficult because fewer past employers are willing to disclose adverse information concerning any prior employee. This is nowhere more true, of course, than with a candidate suspected of being willing to cause trouble.

It must also be remembered that even with the best will in the world, *most referees are inadequately qualified to form an opinion as to the likelihood of a candidate's success in a new and more demanding role.*

A referee may be trusted to verify the facts of a candidate's past employment. Beyond that, however, most opinions need to be discounted.

The value of reference checking lies in using it to confirm—or at least discuss—the strengths and weaknesses identified by a skilled, knowledgeable interviewer.

#7: THE FALLACY OF THE "SCIENTIFIC" TEST

"She got such good test results, we just had to hire her."

Psychological testing has a part to play in management evaluation, but has failed to provide the panacea promised in its 1950s heyday.

The problem with most popular forms of psychological testing offered to industry is not merely that the results are highly unreliable, but that sophisticated test takers become adept in faking "correct" answers, thus attaining so-called executive profiles. In consequence, such tests tend to be remarkably poor predictors of executive success.

Are *any* tests reliable. Yes, experts agree that "projective tests" (like the famed Rorschach Inkblot test, or the Wareham/McMurry Incomplete Sentence Blank), which call for the candidate to reveal his or her personality by psychological projection, can be invaluable when properly administered and analyzed by a qualified practitioner. Because these tests do call for skilled interpretation, however, they have not enjoyed wide use in industry.

It is also well to note that some personnel psychologists are more skilled interpreters than others, just as in medicine some doctors are better diagnosticians than others. In all, testing has been an art and not a science.

THE RIGHT WAY TO SET ABOUT SIZING UP AN EXECUTIVE

Sizing up an executive can be compared to playing a game of chess. The players use the same board, start with the same number of identical pieces, and everything is out in the open to be seen, studied, and analyzed. Somehow, the better player always wins—not because he's necessarily a more intelligent or creative person—but because as he contemplates the board, he reaches back behind his eyes and calls upon a better *understanding* of the game.

So, too, in the game of sizing up an executive, you must first begin by forgetting all about the psyche of the person you are trying to evaluate, and establishing an informed understanding—an intellectual framework—inside *your* head. Then, later, when you sit down to conduct an interview, you'll be ahead of the game, even before you make your first move.

3

THE
TEN ELEMENTS
THAT COMPRISE
THE ANATOMY
OF GREAT EXECUTIVES

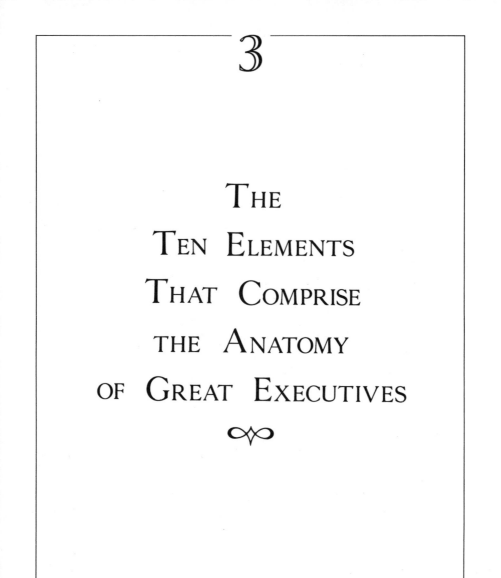

Success as an executive requires the presence of many qualities—whereas failure will proceed from the absence of merely one of them.

DR. ROBERT N. MCMURRY

WHAT YOU NEED TO KNOW TO UNDERSTAND AN EXECUTIVE

(OR ANYONE, FOR THAT MATTER)

LET'S BEGIN WITH A QUICK OVERVIEW...

AN EXECUTIVE
(OR ANYONE FOR THAT MATTER)
IS AN **ENERGY SYSTEM**

WITH A MIND

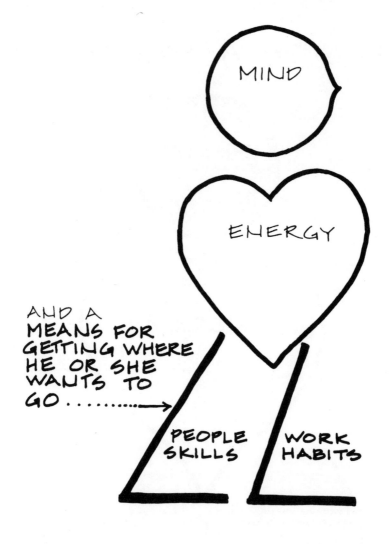

AND IDEALLY, A HISTORY OF
JOB STABILITY

AN EXECUTIVE ALSO NEEDS
TO HAVE HIS OR HER
HEAD ON STRAIGHT

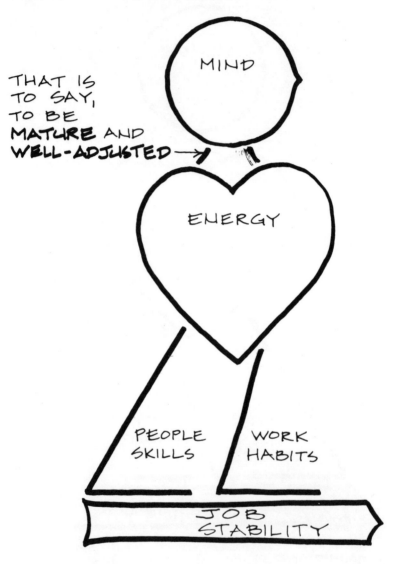

THAT IS
TO SAY,
TO BE
MATURE AND
WELL-ADJUSTED →

TO IDENTIFY A GREAT
EXECUTIVE YOU MUST
EVALUATE THESE QUALITIES
HOWEVER...

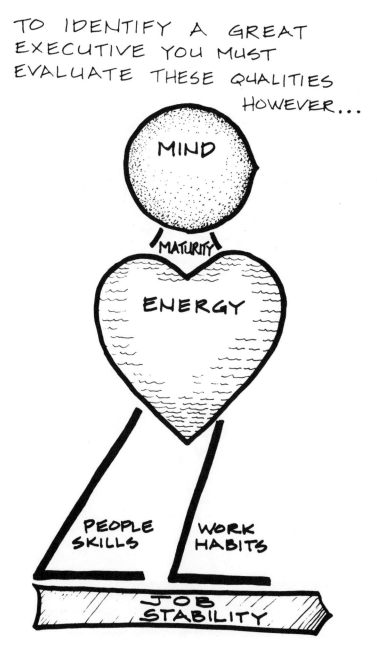

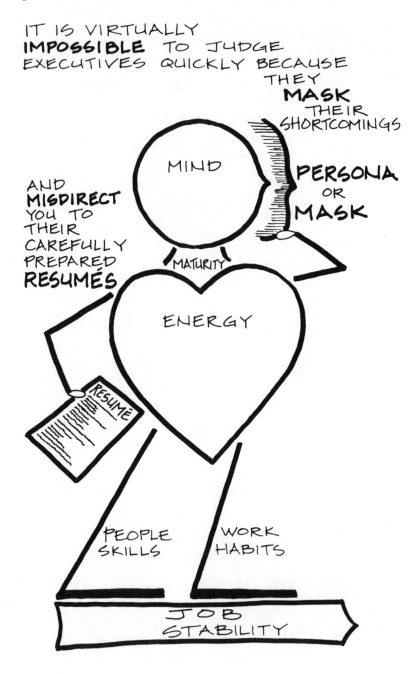

TO SIZE UP AN EXECUTIVE
ACCURATELY YOU MUST GO
BEHIND THE MASK AND
EVALUATE THE THINGS THAT
REALLY
MATTER
MOST

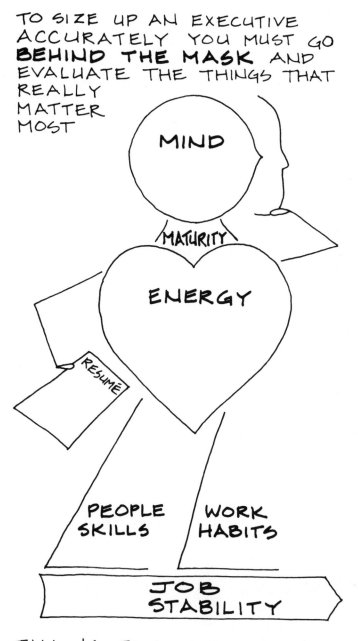

THAT'S THE OVERVIEW
NOW, LET'S LOOK AGAIN,
THIS TIME IN MORE DETAIL.

ELEMENT #1

THE PERSONA OR MASK

No mask like truth to cover lies,
As to go naked is the best disguise.
WILLIAM CONGREVE

Oscar Wilde said that "it would be a terrible world if everybody told the truth, for things are bad enough already with everyone going around telling lies." This aphorism is witty because it is accurate. Most people—you and me included—present a face to the world that seldom reflects our underlying feelings. The Greeks called this face the *persona*. Psychologists often call it a facade, or mask.

The mask we show is intended to perform at least three functions:

- Hide our deficiencies. This is why, despite the prevalence of mental illness, you seldom seem to meet deranged people (except if you live in New York, of course).
- Conceal our antagonisms. Thus, humans are the only animals capable of jesting—apparently amicably—with individuals whom they are actually scheming to kill.
- Win our acceptance by others.

Different people present different facades under different circumstances, and common facades include:

The nice guy
The tough leader
The patrician gentleman
The loyal servant
The go-getter
The urbane corporate executive
The serene, far-seeing elder.

Lucretius, who lived during the first century B.C., realized that the face we present to the world seldom accords with the personality behind it, and wrote:

So it is more useful to watch a man in times of peril, and in adversity to discern what kind of man he is; for then at last words of truth are drawn from the depths of his heart, and the mask is torn off, reality remains.

As a practical matter, however, we seldom have the opportunity to see a person in times of peril. Thus a more useful technique is to apply what I call the principle of the opposite image.

THE PRINCIPLE OF THE OPPOSITE IMAGE

> *Outside noisy, inside empty.*
> CHINESE PROVERB

In presenting a particular facade, many people, like many poker players, are motivated to present an image that is the opposite of the hand they have been dealt:

A person will often present a facade founded upon the aspect of his or her personality that he/she most fears—or knows—to be missing.

Accordingly:
    The bully is often a coward.
    The gentleman is often a cad.
    The clown is often suicidal.
You might note that this principle holds especially true in corporate life, where survival and advancement often seem to demand the projection of false images. Thus:

- The apparently urbane corporate executive often turns out to be incredibly naive.
- The loyal servant is often a duplicitous Uriah Heep.
- The charming salesperson is often a badly adjusted and fundamentally hostile person.

- The country hayseed is likely to prove a very smart operator.
- The macho leader is often a very frightened fellow.

The clear moral is that it is most unwise to rely upon first impressions when evaluating people, for the persona you see—especially at a first meeting—will probably prove to be quite false. Better to cultivate the habit of analyzing the persona that a person projects by asking yourself:

> *What is the impression that this individual takes the greatest trouble to convey to me?*

Then, until you discover more, work on the assumption that the real person may likely turn out to be the exact opposite of this facade.

Now, let's get on to examine the elements behind the mask that comprise the real person.

ELEMENT # 2

ENERGY

Why some people have energy to spare —and some seem to have none

> *Hell is full of the talented, but Heaven of the energetic.*
> JEANNE-FRANÇOISE DE CHANTAL

An executive—or anyone else for that matter—can be defined as an energy system.

We are *born* with an innate level of energy. Energy can be defined to include hungers, drives, aggressions, anxieties, and libidinous impulses. An energy level is inherited, and cannot much be altered.

- *Some people have a lot of energy.* These people are usually very *active.* They are always doing things. Even when they go on holiday they like to remain active, playing tennis, swimming, or somesuch. Or, as they lie on the beach, they make telephone calls on a cellular phone. Most tycoons have a lot of energy. These people have been called *Type A's*.

- *Some people don't seem to have much energy at all.* They can be characterized as *passive*. They can enjoy the quieter, more subtle and reflective pleasures of life. These people have been called *Type B's*.

Most of us fall somewhere on a continuum between these two extremes. However,

- Some small percentage of people swing between the two extremes, buoyant and active one day, yet depressed and passive the next. These people have been called *manic depressives,* or, more recently, sufferers of "Bipolar Affective Disorder" (BAD).

The problem we human beings face is to find satisfying and socially acceptable ways of channeling our energies.

THE MIND DETERMINES HOW TO CHANNEL THAT ENERGY

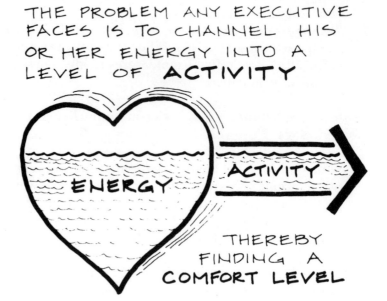

THE PROBLEM ANY EXECUTIVE
FACES IS TO CHANNEL HIS
OR HER ENERGY INTO A
LEVEL OF **ACTIVITY**

ENERGY

ACTIVITY

THEREBY
FINDING A
COMFORT LEVEL

Thus, in our daily lives, we seek a level of activity to match our energy level, and we gravitate to a *point of comfort* or comfort level. Some psychologists also refer to this as the point of least discomfort!

A *longer-term* point of comfort must also be attained. We'll look at this subject in more detail later.

ELEMENT #3

VALUES AND THE PSYCHIC CONTRACT

*Why people seem to behave irrationally
—yet are really very predictable*

> *Humanity is held apart by dogmas
> and statements of truth, and
> attempts to define Humanity are
> drawn together by warm-hearted
> conduct. And yet the conduct we
> approve of often rests upon dogmas
> which we do not approve. The
> dogmas then are as important as
> the conduct.*
> JOHN JAY CHAPMAN

Values are the prime determinants of human behavior, and each of us carries his or her own unique system of values.

- A value is the esteem we assign to an *idea*. Values are concepts, notions, and opinions—not facts. No one can *prove* his or her values to be correct, or superior.
- A value *system* may be defined as the structuring of person's beliefs within his or her cognitive framework. A value system is akin to the software that drives a computer. The value system is wholly or significantly responsible for a person's
  Goals
  Cognitive processes
  Work habits
  Compatibility with others
  Capacity to adjust to a changing world.

Our values are conditioned into us by authority figures, especially our parents. Logic plays little or no part, and we mostly remain unconscious of the processes by which our value system becomes instilled.

THE MIND
COMPRISES MANY ELEMENTS

VALUE SYSTEM

NONE IS MORE CRUCIAL THAN THE **VALUE SYSTEM** BECAUSE THIS IS THE PRIME DETERMINANT OF BEHAVIOR

- Related beliefs become clustered together in constellations within the value system. Thus, if I am a political conservative, I will probably believe in capitalism, the efficacy and goodness of the private school system, and capital punishment.
- Our values are often highly inconsistent. New values—acquired from disparate sources at different periods of our lives—become superimposed upon old values. (As, say, in the case of the "limousine liberal" children who turned to communism in pre-Gorbachev times.) The new values appear to govern attitudes and behavior, but the old values remain in the unconscious and continue to exercise considerable sway. People thereby

often hold violently conflicting standards. Rational discussion rarely permits us to identify and resolve these kinds of inconsistencies, because:

> The values were usually acquired from authority figures, and continue to be held in the unconscious.
> To question those values may undermine the individual's whole philosophy of life, leaving him unbearably anxious.
> The existence of a double standards and hypocrisy, simply cannot be faced, so we:

>> Rationalize virtually any inconsistency. And, the more intelligent the person, the greater the ability to rationalize.
>> Become defensive and angry if the inconsistency is pointed out. Hence the wisdom in the adage, "There's nothing wrong with teenagers that reasoning with them won't aggravate."

Thus, humankind may:

- Preach against adultery, yet enjoy the services of a prostitute or gigolo.
- Be pious on the Sabbath [or Sunday], yet be deceitful on weekdays.
- Champion freedom as an idea, yet deplore it in actual practice.
- The earlier our values are acquired, the greater their power. Early values become the *voice of conscience.* This voice governs our behavior, usually without our awareness, by inflicting subtle—and not so subtle—rewards and punishments. We feel good when we do what conscience tells us, and bad when we don't.

The Paradox of Values.   Most people cherish what they imagine to be an almost sacred right to hold and live by a system of values that springs from invalid and conflicting beliefs. They do so, believing that to live in accordance with one's beliefs bestows integrity, gives meaning to life, and makes us free. *The exact opposite, however, is more likely to be the*

THE
VOICE OF CONSCIENCE
IS A KEY ELEMENT
IN THE VALUE SYSTEM
BECAUSE IT **COMPELS** THE
EXECUTIVE TO **OBEY** THE
VALUE SYSTEM OR
**BE PUNISHED WITH
GUILTY FEELINGS**

VALUES

VOICE OF CONSCIENCE

case. People are mostly prisoners trapped within the cage of their own beliefs, yet unaware of any restraint.

HOW OUR VALUES GOVERN OUR LIVES

We mostly acquire our values from our parents. They typically instill the value system of the prevailing culture. In all, then, our parents set up our lifetime destinies by providing our

- Genes and genetic programming
- Place in the family
- Name
- Religion
- Culture, environment, and citizenship

- Immediate neighborhood and peer group
- Value system and goals
- Rewards and punishments
- Emotional climate
- Educational opportunities
- Television viewing opportunities.

THE PSYCHIC CONTRACT

The voice of conscience establishes and guides our destinies by means of a *psychic contract,* comprising:

The Prime Parental Directive. Parental expectations are often encapsulated in one or two simple injunctions. Thus:

- Conformist parents will likely script their offspring to "be good and do what you are told."
- Achieving parents urge their kids to "be the best in all you do."
- Security-minded parents say, "Be careful, save money, and never go into debt."

The General Contract. As we grow we absorb the values of our parents, and are conditioned to improve (albeit marginally) upon their attainments. We strike a psychic contract with them whereby "success" in life is defined by the attainment of a similar social positioning, which we later embark upon attaining, sometimes very consciously, but often entirely unconsciously.

- *The guiding criteria of success.* Conscience is the usual arbiter of success in life. We think we try to live up to our personal principles, but in reality we unconsciously measure success in terms of milestones and standards instilled by our parents.
- *The lifestyle expectation.* As a rule of thumb, about three quarters or more of people in westernized culture seek first to equal, then marginally to improve upon the lifestyle or status level perceived to exist in the childhood home.

The Central Life Interest.   The guiding criteria of success, and the lifestyle expectation, usually blend to comprise the activity—or *central life interest*—to which we devote our minds and energies. For some people, this will mean pursuing business success; for others, it may entail building a happy family life and paying down the mortgage. And so on.

The Golden Spur.   Motivation, like the grit that makes the pearl in the oyster, usually springs from some sense of deprivation. The psychologist Carl Jung said that we are powerfully motivated by the unfulfilled ambitions of our parents. I call this kind of motivation a *Golden Spur.* Usually it lies buried in the unconscious, from where it provokes a very conscious *burning desire,* which may take the form of wanting to succeed where our parents did not. Accordingly, the answer to the question of why the former tennis star Chrissie Evert labored so long at the game, and accomplished so much, seems related to the fact that her father was a professional tennis coach. By excelling in the game, she validated both of their lives.

To be raised in a poor or disadvantaged home can also spur achievement, especially if the child enjoyed a secure, sound, happy, loving relationship with the parents. Such children grow up feeling secure within themselves, and therefore likely to be competent performers at whatever they choose. They are also likely to be driven by a powerful sense of social inferiority, and therefore want to show great achievement. Lee Iacocca, for example, enjoyed a very close, happy relationship with his parents, but bridled at the discrimination that was directed against him and his family for being Italian immigrants.

Or consider the case of the black politician, the Reverend Jesse Jackson, who ran for president of the United States. Mr. Jackson, an illegitimate child, lived with his mother on "the wrong side of town." His father, an outwardly respectable black businessman, paid clandestine visits to Jesse's mother during the week, but lived with his wife and *their* children on the right side of town. Accordingly, Jesse Jackson developed a burning desire to be seen, to be respectable, to be approved of, to be *somebody.* His quest for the

White House can thus be viewed as an unconscious wish to take his rightful place in that most respectable house on the other side of town.

The Phaeton Force.   In Greek mythology, Phaeton, son of Apollo the Sun God, seeking to win status among his peers, persuades his reluctant father to let him ride the chariot of the sun across the sky. Phaeton underestimates his ability to manage the fiery horses that pull the chariot, however, and without Apollo's weight in the chariot, and his firm hand to guide them, the horses race away, smashing the chariot and tossing Phaeton to his death.

In real life, indulged children often develop unrealistic status needs, which they seek to fulfill with ultimately disastrous consequences. Indeed, the need for status—as opposed to achievement—often signals immaturity and unrealism. Thus, failed auto "mogul" John DeLorean, who lived with his indulgent mother till age twenty-eight, finally set out to create and market a dream car, only to meet with spectacular failure.

The Culminating Achievement.
Fulfillment of the psychic contract may also be measured in terms of a *culminating achievement,* a *specific quantifiable event,* often related to the unfulfilled ambition of the person's parents. For example, a person whose father wanted but failed to become a millionaire—pretty small cheese these days!—might be driven to attain this goal.

The culminating achievement must often be realized by a specific age, relating to:

- the age of the parents as perceived by the growing child;
- a time frame specified by one or both parents ("If you haven't made it by age forty, then you're no child of mine");
- the ages and achievements of siblings or peers;
- the lifetime of one or both parents (the achievement might not count if the parents are not alive to recognize it).

Examples of culminating achievements might include:

- founding a business;
- being appointed senior officer of a public company;
- being appointed university professor;
- having a book published;
- owning a small mortgage-free home;
- acquiring a very large, albeit heavily mortgaged home;
- raising a conformist child, and having it graduate from a socially acceptable college or university.

Winning and Losing.   The person who makes good on his or her psychic contract is a winner. The person who fails to make good is a loser.

> A person might be rich and prosperous, yet, if he failed to fulfill the psychic contract—say by failing to outperform his even more prosperous parents—he is still a loser.

> Equally, a person might meet with only very modest success by material standards, yet so long as this enabled her to fulfill the psychic contract, she would judge herself to be a winner.

The Poisonous Override.   Sometimes a badly adjusted parent may poison a contract by adding an override to the prime parental directive. Such overrides might include:

> "Do your very best—but never get it right."
> "Make a lot of money—and kill yourself in the process."
> "Achieve—but never enjoy sufficient peace of mind to savor your accomplishments."

The Payoff.   Every contract has a payoff. Normally a winning payoff is to gain your freedom and happily set about enjoying the rest of your life. The losers' usual payoff is to suffer guilty feelings, and to believe they've let everyone down, including themselves. A losing payoff might even call for the loser to fall upon some kind of sword.

In the poisoned contract, a "winning" payoff involves being made to feel unworthy of success—and, therefore, compelled to engage in acts of self-sabotage.

ELEMENT #4

CONSCIOUS GOALS
AND HIDDEN AGENDAS

If you don't know where you're going, you'll probably wind up somewhere else.
LAURENCE J. PETER

Our goals can be divided into two broad categories: (a) underlying drives, and (b) resultant needs.

UNDERLYING DRIVES

Underlying drives spring from not one, but two underlying voices: the voice of *conscience* and the voice of *self.*

The voice of self is the still, small, unique, central voice that we hear within us, but which, alas, we often fail to heed. The role of this voice is to guide us in our quest to realize our full potential.

The voice of conscience is the voice of parents and authority figures from the past who instilled the value system, thereby setting up the "family destiny," in terms of a psychic contract and a culminating achievement. It is the voice that seeks to govern that destiny and police that contract!

RESULTANT NEEDS

The needs that spring from our underlying drives may be divided into three categories: financial, societal, and psychological.

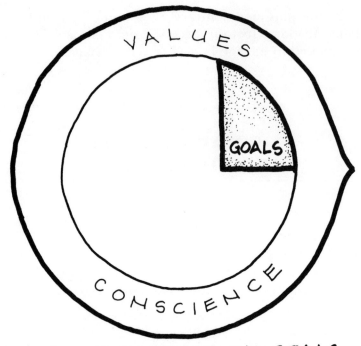

OUR VALUES DETERMINE OUR **GOALS**

GOALS CAN
BE DIVIDED
INTO TWO
CATEGORIES:

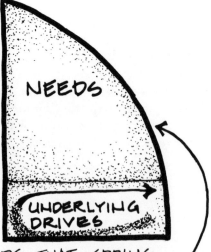

1. UNDERLYING
   DRIVES

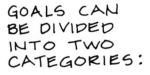

2. AND THE NEEDS THAT SPRING
   FROM THESE UNDERLYING DRIVES

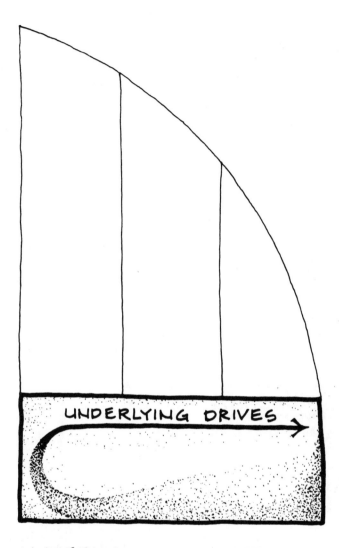

UNDERLYING DRIVES
(OF WHICH WE ARE OFTEN
UNCONSCIOUS) ARE USUALLY THE
MOST POWERFUL DRIVING FORCES

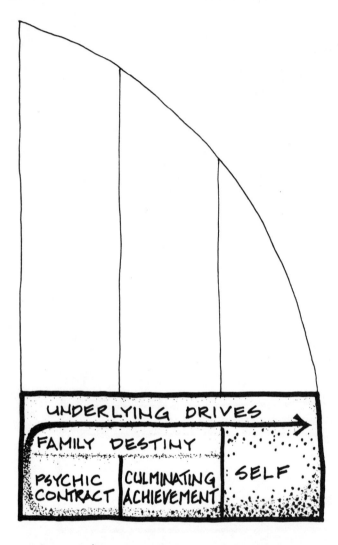

THE THREE MOST IMPORTANT
UNDERLYING DRIVES ARE:

1. THE TERMS OF THE PSYCHIC CONTRACT
2. THE QUEST FOR THE CULMINATING
   ACHIEVEMENT
3. THE DRIVE TO BECOME ONESELF

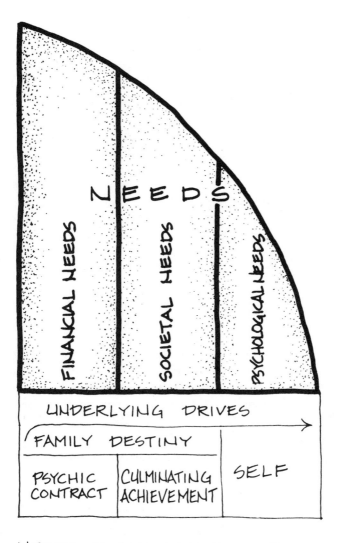

NEEDS CAN BE DIVIDED INTO
THREE CATEGORIES:

1. FINANCIAL

2. SOCIETAL

3. PSYCHOLOGICAL

FINANCIAL

From a practical point of view, a vital financial need is for the *income* to maintain a particular lifestyle.

People with apparently similar lifestyles—neighbors with identical houses, cars, tuition bills, and so on—may in fact have vastly differing income needs:

- One family may enjoy inherited wealth, and have no mortgage or car leases to pay.
- The other family may have gone heavily into debt in order to live in the same well-to-do neighborhood.

Hence Lewis Carroll's observation:

> "A slow sort of country!" said the Queen. "Now, *here*, you see, it takes all the running you can do to keep in the same place. If you want to get somewhere else, you must run at least twice as fast as that!"

The financial comfort level normally rises and falls during a person's life. We need little in our teens and twenties, and comparatively little when starting out in life. The comfort level usually rises as we strive to get up in the world, educate our children, and stretch to establish and maintain higher and higher lifestyles, thereby keeping up with the Joneses. Later, as children leave home and inflation takes care of the mortgage, income needs tend to fall—thus losing the power to drive a person to earn.

SOCIETAL

Societal needs reflect the drive to fulfill the lifestyle expectation clause in the psychic contract. This is not just a matter of money, but of finding a place in a social structure or hierarchy. For convenience sake we may divide that hierarchy into at least four categories:

Craftsman
Merchant
Professional
Artist

Some families are happy to remain at one level for several generations. More frequently, in westernized culture where upward mobility is much prized, the psychic contract has called for each generation to edge its way up the totem pole:

- The craftsman raises his child to become a well-to-do shopkeeper. "My daughter, who has her own thriving business!"
- The businessperson raises her child to become an esteemed professional. "My son the doctor!"
- The offspring of the professional, having enjoyed many advantages, comes naturally to value art above all else. "My child, the rock star!"

PSYCHOLOGICAL

Psychological needs tend to spring from the values inculcated in the home, and the psychic contract. Certain of our needs—such as those for money, food, and shelter—vary during our lives. However, other underlying needs—such as the needs for power, autonomy, and affection—remain fairly constant.

Key psychological needs and consequent underlying fears include:

Security: Wanting to establish and maintain an economic niche that cannot easily be unsettled in the event of recession. Underlying fear of falling back into poverty.

Status: Wants to be seen and is concerned with status-conferring objects, neighborhood, schools, occupations. Underlying feelings of inadequacy and inferiority.

Power: Seeks power, authority, and influence over the lives and behavior of others. Underlying fear of helplessness.

Investigation: Wants to discover what makes things work. Wants to get at the truth. Underlying fear that the truth may be withheld.

Achievement: Wanting to show outstanding accomplishment. In fact, the high-need achiever may also be seeking attention and acceptance. Underlying fear of failure.

Service: Wanting to serve or help others. To work in the community and improve the lives of others. Underlying need for approval.

Approval: Wanting not just to serve, but to be seen to have served, and to be approved of for having done the right thing. Underlying fear of being punished for doing the wrong thing.

Acceptance: Concern with social approval and acceptance. A common need of many immigrants, who may completely embrace the values of a new culture in order to win acceptance. Underlying fear of rejection.

Affiliation: Wants to mix with others, to share good feelings and camaraderie. Underlying fear of loneliness.

Autonomy: Wants to be in full control of own destiny. A common need of many small entrepreneurs. Does not want to be controlled or directed by others. Underlying fear of losing a sense of identity.

Perfection: Wants to be seen as flawless, immaculate, impeccable, perfect. A perfectionist has been fairly accurately described as a person who takes great pains, and gives them to others. Perfectionists are virtually always attempting to overcome an emotional shortcoming, imagined or otherwise. Underlying fear of revealing emotional weaknesses and blemishes.

THE DRIVE TO BECOME ONESELF

Not all needs spring from parental programming. Some are intrinsic to the person, a part of his or her authentic self, and not just clauses in the psychic contract. They are:

Self-improvement: Wants to grow as a person, and realize full potential. Abraham Maslow called this the need to self-actualize. The need for self-improvement is very strong in entrepreneurs and, probably, most creative people. It is *not* a strong need in all people. It probably is fairly strong in *you,* however, dear reader, for this book might not otherwise be in your hands.

Meaning: Concern to find meaning in life, and to feel that all our strivings are not futile. This is related to the need for self-improvement.

THE KEY COMFORT LEVELS

In considering a person's goals it is therefore smart to focus on the four key comfort levels, as well as the two key underlying needs.

COMFORT LEVELS

1. Physical energy level.
2. Financial comfort level.
3. Lifestyle expectation.
4. Key psychological needs.

NEEDS

1. Underlying psychic contract.
2. Drive to self-actualize.

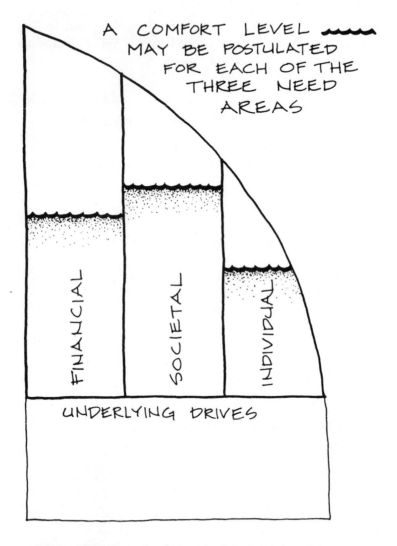

A COMFORT LEVEL ~~~~ MAY BE POSTULATED FOR EACH OF THE THREE NEED AREAS

FINANCIAL

SOCIETAL

INDIVIDUAL

UNDERLYING DRIVES

THE DRIVE AND ENERGY TO KEEP PUSHING BECOME LESSENED WHEN A SPECIFIC COMFORT LEVEL IS ATTAINED

THUS, WHEN CONTEMPLATING A PERSON'S **OVERALL** LEVEL OF COMFORT, WE MUST EXAMINE

4 KEY LEVELS

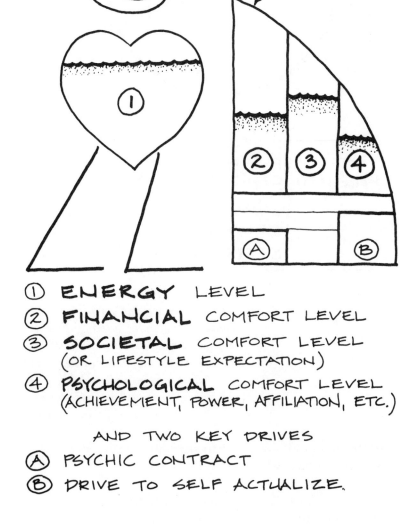

① **ENERGY** LEVEL

② **FINANCIAL** COMFORT LEVEL

③ **SOCIETAL** COMFORT LEVEL
(OR LIFESTYLE EXPECTATION)

④ **PSYCHOLOGICAL** COMFORT LEVEL
(ACHIEVEMENT, POWER, AFFILIATION, ETC.)

AND TWO KEY DRIVES

Ⓐ PSYCHIC CONTRACT

Ⓑ DRIVE TO SELF ACTUALIZE.

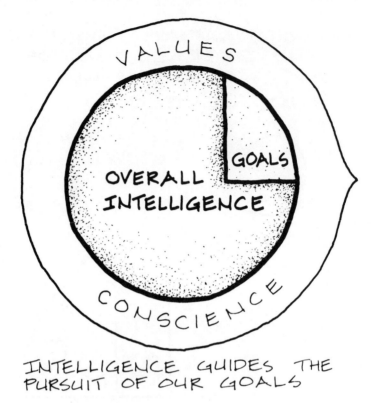

INTELLIGENCE GUIDES THE
PURSUIT OF OUR GOALS

ELEMENT # 5

INTELLIGENCE

> *Intelligence is not something
> possessed once and for all. It is in
> constant process of forming, and its
> retention requires constant alertness
> in observing consequences, and
> open-minded will to learn and
> courage in readjustment.*
> JOHN DEWEY

To attain our goals we need to use our intelligence.
Intelligence has two basic definitions:

- Information itself, a body of knowledge.
- The ability to process information accurately, thereby
  resolving problems and expanding knowledge.

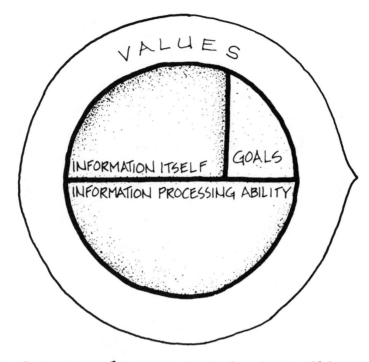

OVERALL INTELLIGENCE COMPRISES
TWO ELEMENTS:

1. **INFORMATION** ITSELF

2. THE ABILITY TO GATHER, STORE,
   AND **PROCESS** THAT INFORMATION

Overall intelligence may thus be thought of as comprising the two major elements of knowledge (or information) and information-processing ability. Let's look at these elements in more detail.

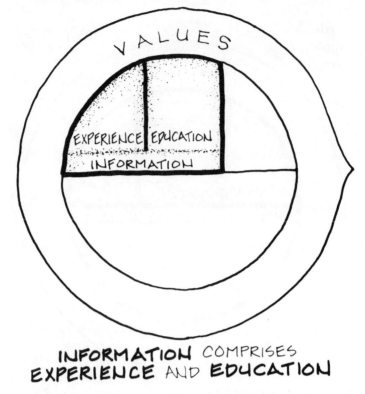

INFORMATION COMPRISES
EXPERIENCE AND **EDUCATION**

KNOWLEDGE OR INFORMATION

By virtue of genetic memory we may be born with some preexisting knowledge. However, for the most part, knowledge must be *acquired* by means of (a) education and (b) experience.

EDUCATION

> *The difference between
> intelligence and education is this:
> intelligence will make you a good living.*
> CHARLES F. KETTERING

When we talk of education, we normally mean the knowledge and learning ability acquired and developed during formal schooling. Unfortunately, much education merely rewards the development of the kind of knowledge and reasoning needed to pass multiple choice tests. Thus, a degree or diploma—or a flotilla of degrees and diplomas— may signify only the holder's capacity to acquire a body of knowledge for sufficient length of time to complete a series of relatively straightforward tests. This may not be the same as a truly developed overall intelligence, which the possessor can use to make decisions calling for qualities of imagination and judgment.

EXPERIENCE

> *Experience is not what happens to*
> *a man, it is what a man does*
> *with what happens to him.*
> ALDOUS HUXLEY

Experience may be defined as what we learn—intellectually and emotionally—from the sum of the challenges and information-gathering opportunities to which we are exposed. A person's experience should thus add to his or her knowledge, and information-processing abilities. Such experience enhances an executive's know-how or fund of *tacit knowledge*—the body of "inside" practical information absorbed during a career. Such experience also ideally fosters emotional growth, and improves the capacity to react positively and quickly in new and even more demanding situations.

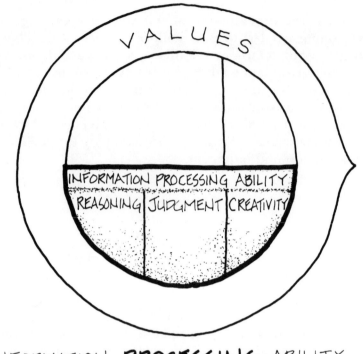

INFORMATION **PROCESSING** ABILITY
COMPRISES **REASONING, JUDGMENT,**
AND **CREATIVITY**

THE CAPACITY TO
PROCESS INFORMATION

We accomplish this by means of (a) reasoning ability, (b) judgment, and (c) creativity. Let's look at these three faculties in more detail.

REASONING ABILITY

> *Those who desire to rise high must*
> *renounce the omnipotence of clear thinking,*
> *belief in the absolute power of logic.*
> ALEXIS CARREL

Reasoning ability may be defined as the capacity to solve problems methodically and quickly, within a logical frame-

work. In a business situation, such ability is typically measured by tests of numerical reasoning, verbal reasoning,
and, often, pictorial reasoning.

Many people fail to appreciate that the ability to reason is merely one element of intelligence. A person may
attain high scores on reasoning tests, yet possess a low
overall intelligence. Other people, who show a mediocre
reasoning ability, may nonetheless show a high overall
intelligence as measured by their ability to make significant achievements. Many great scientists have fit this
description.

JUDGMENT

*All the wise men were on one side,
and all the fools were on the other . . .
And, be damned, Sir, all the fools were right!*
DUKE OF WELLINGTON

Judgment is a higher order of skill than mere reasoning,
for it involves:

1. weighing the problem at hand;
2. scanning all knowledge and experience—much of it
    stored in the unconscious mind—in order to dis-
    cover which set of principles might render the best
    solution;
3. applying logic and reason to the problem in terms
    of those principles;
4. monitoring the result attained, and if it seems unac-
    ceptable, going back into the unconscious to bring
    forth and apply yet another set of principles.

Judgment is a function of education and experience, as
well as reasoning, logic, and intuition. Reasoning is using
logic to examine all the elements of a puzzle, and working
out the correct answer. Judgment is the infinitely more
refined capacity of considering an ambiguous situation,
and using both logic and intuition to make a really good
guess.

CREATIVITY

> *Personally, I would rather have written*
> Alice in Wonderland *than the*
> *whole* Encyclopaedia Britannica.
> STEPHEN LEACOCK

Creativity might be defined as judgment plus imagination. It is the capacity to examine and process data, make new connections, and come up with fresh ideas and solutions. Creativity is not much related to straightforward reasoning ability. Indeed, it has been found time and again that highly creative people were often only mediocre students. The great strength of a creative person is the capacity to discard old rules and principles, and fashion new rules. An important part of the creative person's capacity to achieve this lies in having built a rich body of diverse information in his or her unconscious. Thus, creative people often enjoy wide interests. However, though creativity can be developed, it nonetheless seems to be mostly innate, which is to say you either have it or you don't. Creativity engages a process that harnesses both the conscious and the unconscious elements of the mind. A problem is approached consciously, but processed unconsciously.

The esteemed psychologist Rollo May, a very creative person himself, observed that the test of a truly creative solution is that it possesses an elegance that even its discoverer knows could not have been assembled consciously. The work of Anton Bruckner seems to meet this test, as witness his reply when asked, "Master, how did you think of the divine motif for your Ninth Symphony?" "Well, it was like this," Bruckner replied. "I walked up the Kahlberg and when it got hot and I got hungry, I sat down by a little brook and unpacked my Swiss cheese. And, just as I open the greasy paper, that darn tune pops into my head!"

VALUES AND INTELLIGENCE

Keep in mind that intelligence is also a function of values, for our values determine the things that we choose to pay attention to, along with how hard we will want to work at them. If education and intelligence are prized within a home, then those brought up within that home are likely to become more intelligent than might otherwise have been the case, for the pursuit of knowledge will enhance the hopper of information that a person acquires, as well as his or her capacity to process that information. And if, as is likely, that person develops an ego involvement in being intelligent, then he or she will probably work to strengthen the information-processing mechanisms.

THIS IS THE FRAMEWORK FOR EVALUATING
THE MIND OF AN EXECUTIVE

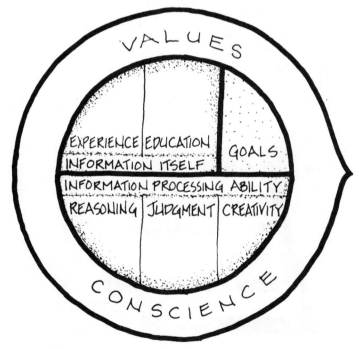

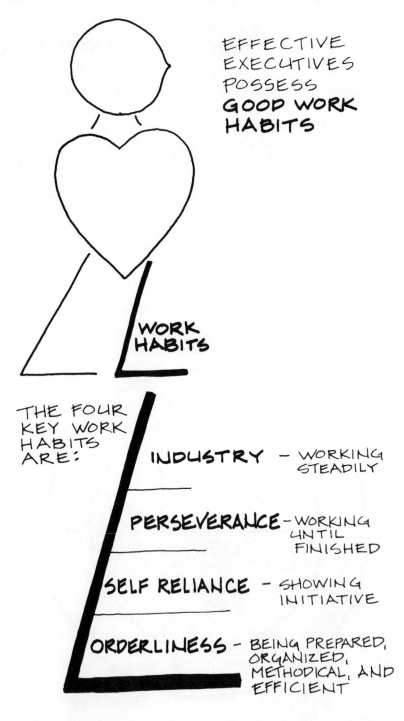

EFFECTIVE
EXECUTIVES
POSSESS
**GOOD WORK
HABITS**

**WORK
HABITS**

THE FOUR
KEY WORK
HABITS
ARE:

INDUSTRY – WORKING
STEADILY

PERSEVERANCE – WORKING
UNTIL
FINISHED

SELF RELIANCE – SHOWING
INITIATIVE

ORDERLINESS – BEING PREPARED,
ORGANIZED,
METHODICAL, AND
EFFICIENT

ELEMENT # 6

WORK HABITS

Most people like hard work.
Particularly when they're paying for it.
FRANKLIN P. JONES

The four key work habits of an executive are: Industry, Perseverance, Self Reliance, and Orderliness.

1. INDUSTRY

I go on working for the same
reason a hen goes on laying eggs.
H. L. MENCKEN

Industry may be defined as the habit of working steadily, productively, voluntarily, and conscientiously, at whatever job is assigned. The industrious person becomes uncomfortable if not productively engaged.

If the power to work hard is not talent, it is certainly the best possible substitute, for, as Ernest Newman has noted:

> The great composer does not set to work because he is inspired, but becomes inspired because he is working. Beethoven, Wagner, Bach, and Mozart settled down day after day to the job in hand with as much regularity as an accountant settles down each day to his figures. They didn't waste time waiting for inspiration.

Great executives work hard because they are driven by the voice of conscience. They also work to fulfill themselves—or their *selves!* They share the sentiment of Jose Ortega y Gasset, who wrote: "An *unemployed* existence is a worse negation of life than death itself. Because to live means to have something definite to do—a mission to fulfill—and in the measure in which we avoid setting our life to something, we make it empty. Human life, by its very nature has to be dedicated to something."

Sometimes people see work as akin to an addiction, and, indeed, sometimes it is. More frequently, however, work is a means of becoming and staying well adjusted. "Work is a callus against grief," said Cicero. And, consider Sigmund Freud's advice: "No other technique for the conduct of life attaches the individual so firmly to reality as laying emphasis on work; for his work at least gives him a secure place in a portion of reality, in the human community."

Nothing is really work unless you would rather be doing something else.

2. PERSEVERANCE

*Let me tell you the secret
that has led me to my goal.
My strength lies solely in my tenacity.*
LOUIS PASTEUR

To persevere is simply to press on in an activity in the face of obstacles, until the objective is attained.

It is one thing to work hard at something, and quite another to see it to completion. The habit of perseverance is usually deeply ingrained in great executives, for like great athletes, they realize that the prize will only be theirs if they can outlast the competition. As the fighter Jimmy Corbett remarked, "To become champion, fight one more round."

Perseverance is the habit—and knack—of throwing off that first impulse to give up, and instead, pushing on to discover and develop an interest in the task, then, often, a passion to complete it. Perseverance is a balancing act that involves keeping the goal in mind while also focusing on the task at hand, however mundane that task might seem. As Lafcadio Hearn observed, "All the best work is done the way ants do things—by tiny but untiring and regular additions." But, as Disraeli concluded, we must also keep the ultimate goal in mind: "I have brought myself by long meditation to the conviction that a human being with a settled purpose must accomplish it, and that nothing can resist a will which will stake even existence upon fulfillment."

---

3. SELF-RELIANCE

Taking everything into account,
only one solution becomes me—my own.
ANTONIN G. SERTILLANGES

Self-reliance is the habit of standing on one's own feet and solving one's own problems despite difficulties and oppositions—instead of merely leaning on others.

Life itself is about becoming self-reliant, standing up to others and looking out for ourselves. Self-reliance, like initiative, is the knee-jerk habit of figuring out for yourself what is the best thing to do, and then doing it. It is a habit of the emotions and the head, as much as of behavior. The self-reliant person is a more complete person, and therefore a better executive.

Great executives have to be self-reliant, for most of the time there is simply no one to lean on. Where difficult decisions have to be made, they must ultimately rely upon their own counsel.

---

4. ORDERLINESS

It is not enough to be busy, the
question is: what are we busy about.
HENRY DAVID THOREAU

Orderliness is preparedness; it is the habit of assigning an order, pattern plan, or system to one's work.

The effective executive wants to be freed from routine work, and taking the time to get organized is one of the best ways to help achieve this. The well-organized person has more effective hours in the day, and a clearer head. Organi-.zation is leverage, it is power.

Orderliness reflects a disciplined mind and the potential to think clearly. It is not possible to be well organized without effort, but the effort required is not that great, and it is time well invested. The badly organized person reveals an incapacity for self-discipline, as well as a poor apprecia-tion of the value of time.

The key to being well organized is to set up an efficient work space, establish goals, tasks, priorities, and dead-lines—and to manage one's time. Orderliness is a kind of magic, for it creates time, relieves pressure, and engenders calm self-confidence. The well-organized executive is also more likely to be *lucky*, for, after all, luck is merely prepara-tion meeting opportunity.

One more work habit might also be postulated: Job Stability.

JOB STABILITY

> *The stability of the internal medium is a primary condition for the freedom and independence of certain living bodies in relation to the environment surrounding them.*
> LEÇONS SUR LES PHÉNOMÈNES
> DE LA VIE COMMUNE
> AUX ANIMAUX ET AUX VÉGÉTAUX

Job stability is the habit of remaining on one job for a reasonable length of time. We read a lot about people getting to the top by moving from company to company. In point of fact, however, relatively few successful executives

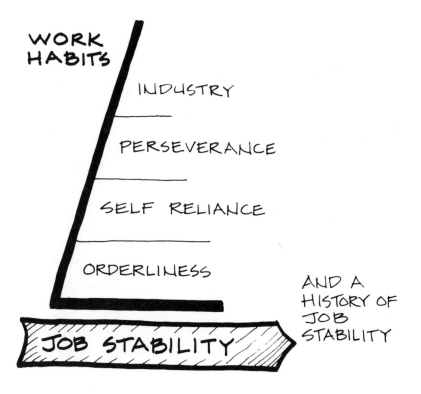

WORK HABITS
INDUSTRY
PERSEVERANCE
SELF RELIANCE
ORDERLINESS

JOB STABILITY

AND A HISTORY OF JOB STABILITY

are job hoppers—for good reason! Employers recognize their strengths and make every effort to keep them happy. A history of job instability, on the other hand, often signals mutual incompatibility. Flitting executives, whatever their strengths, are often badly adjusted people who harbor unrealistic expectations that no employer could ever satisfy— or want to.

From a practical point of view, job stability is important because employers want to hire individuals who hope to build long-term careers. More subtly, however, the savvy employer also realizes that, with some exceptions, job hoppers are likely to be impaired by many more problems than simple lack of tenure.

BEHAVIORAL CHECKLIST #1

Specific Work Behaviors
Demonstrated by Successful Executives

It can be instructive to rate an executive's specific work behaviors with two clusters of behavior routinely displayed by other successful managers.

A. *Resolving.* The point of having an intellect is to take appropriate action in practical everyday situations. A good manager applies his or her intellect to problem solving and decision making. He or she

1. *Evidences know-how.* Shows the expertise, or technical skills, necessary to manage the product, service, or functional discipline.
2. *Shows practical judgment.* Doesn't regularly make unwise, questionable, or naive decisions.
3. *Deals effectively with ambiguity.* Is comfortable in a loosely structured, changing environment, and at ease with relationships, objectives, strategies, performance measures.
4. *Shows flexibity in dealing with change.* Welcomes new ideas and alternatives.
5. *Fixes appropriate priorities.* Tackles important items first. Doesn't get distracted by low-priority issues.
6. *Develops and evaluates alternative problem solutions.* Doesn't opt for the first quick fix or easy way out.
7. *Shows decisiveness.* Is willing to take a point of view and stand behind it.
8. *Acknowledges errors.* Admits to mistakes, errors of judgment, or poor decisions.
9. *Eschews unnecessary rules.* Knows when to bend the rules or throw away the book to expedite results.

B. *Administering.* A good manager appreciates the need for sound "housekeeping." He or she

1. *Sets up an appropriate structure.* Ensures that subordinates

OVERALL, HOW **HARD** —
AND HOW **EFFECTIVELY** —
AN EXECUTIVE WORKS IS A
FUNCTION OF **5** ELEMENTS

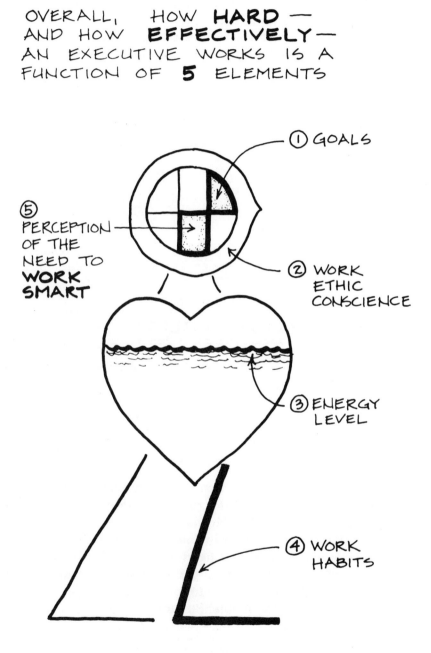

① GOALS

⑤ PERCEPTION OF THE NEED TO **WORK SMART**

② WORK ETHIC CONSCIENCE

③ ENERGY LEVEL

④ WORK HABITS

understand their objectives, responsibilities, and the limits of their authority.

2. *Values objective control.* Uses control systems to monitor unit's progress toward objectives.

3. *Demonstrates orderliness.* Possesses disciplined, organized, well-planned work habits. Anticipates and meets deadlines.

4. *Manages own time effectively.* Is sensitive to how subordinates spend their time.

ELEMENT # 7

PEOPLE SKILLS

> *I will pay more for the ability to deal with people than for any ability under the sun.*
> JOHN D. ROCKEFELLER

The savvy executive is usually a *socially* intelligent executive. He realizes the importance of getting along with people, and knows how to do it. He also develops the requisite *emotional* qualities and hones his *communication* behaviors.

A back-room boffin doesn't need to get on with anyone. A true executive, however, must get along with all manner of people. Specifically, she has to apply her social intelligence to four groups of people: Superiors, Peers, Subordinates, and Customers.

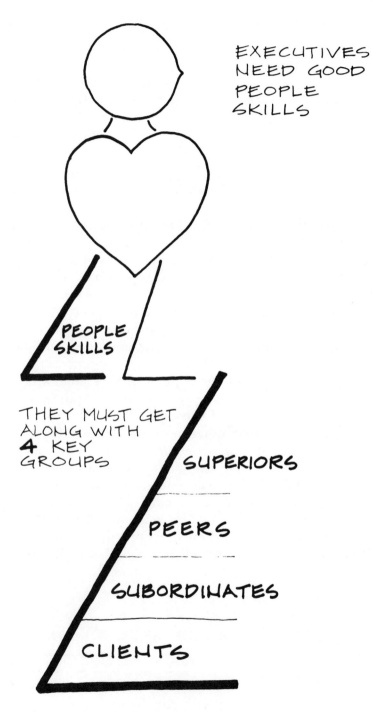

EXECUTIVES
NEED GOOD
PEOPLE
SKILLS

PEOPLE
SKILLS

THEY MUST GET
ALONG WITH
4 KEY
GROUPS

SUPERIORS

PEERS

SUBORDINATES

CLIENTS

SUPERIORS

*Stand not too near the rich man
lest he destroy thee nor too far
away, lest he forget thee.*
ANEURIN BEVAN

The person who can't get along with the boss or the members of the board is seldom going to last in an executive role.

Getting along with the boss entails being able to listen, exchange information, resolve differences, act in accordance with agreed policy, and report back as necessary—all while making the boss look as good as possible: "Better the ass that carries me than the ass that throws me," said Thomas Fuller. The boss is entitled to expect loyalty, of course, not so much to her as to the cause that she represents. The idea, after all, is that both boss and subordinate are pursuing the same goals. When it becomes necessary to disagree and fight for another point of view, then a savvy subordinate will do so, but with tact, confining the discussion to facts, options, and consequences.

The easiest and sometimes most effective way to get on with a boss is to become her clone and slave. Fortunately, this tends to be beyond the ability of most outstanding executives. Indeed, the analects of Confucius tell us that Tzu-Lu asked how to serve the king. The master replied: "Never cheat him: withstand him to the face." This is to be balanced with George Herbert's very practical advice not to follow truth too near the heels lest it dash out thy teeth!

PEERS

*Working with people is hard, but
not impossible.*
PETER DRUCKER

An executive must win the acceptance of his peers if he is to function as a team player. Getting along with peers—or anyone—begins with the realization that this is the *wise* thing to do. Effective executives minimize conflict and do not alienate others unnecessarily. They listen and *hear* the ideas of others. They present their own ideas cogently, and with concern for the feelings of their listener. This is not a matter of being a conformist or an "organization" person, it is simply a matter of common sense. The same common sense that may sometimes dictate a calm refusal to reach an early consensus.

Savvy executives also realize that politics are a fairly normal element of everyday corporate life. Many people find corporate politics distasteful, and it certainly can be. Savvy executives are careful not to be labeled politicians, and shun unseemly politicking. However, they also realize that they must both survive and advance within an essentially political climate. They know that virtually anyone they are currently dealing with may turn up in a position to perform or reject a favor tomorrow. They realize that today's friend may be tomorrow's enemy (and the closer the friend, the more bitter the enemy). They realize that friends come and go but enemies accumulate. They thus choose their enemies carefully, and nurture an ample network of allies. Lord Chesterfield put it well: "In your friendships and in your enmities, let your confidence and your hostilities have certain bounds; make not the former dangerous, nor the latter irreconcilable. For there are strange vicissitudes in business."

SUBORDINATES

*Look over your shoulder now and then
to be sure somebody's following you.*
HENRY GILMER

An executive must gain the respect and following of his or her subordinates. Doing this requires realization that there is *no* one leadership style that will work in all settings. Clarence Randall wrote:

> Leadership, like everything else in life that is vital, finds its source in understanding. To be worthy of manage-

ment responsibility today, a man must have insight into the human heart, for unless he has an awareness of human problems, a sensitivity towards the hopes and aspirations of those whom he supervises, and a capacity for analysis of the emotional forces that motivate their conduct, the projects entrusted to him will not get ahead no matter how often wages are raised.

Savvy executives thus temper their management style to (a) *The demands of the situation.* They may be as autocratic as Attila the Hun himself if leading a platoon in battle, or as democratic as a John F. Kennedy in peacetime. (b) *The intellectual and emotional needs of their followers.* As Ovid said, "Treat a thousand dispositions in a thousand ways." A group of right-wing intellectuals might therefore demand a more rigid leader than perhaps would their left-wing counterparts.

―――――

CUSTOMERS

> *It is a great art,*
> *to know how to sell wind.*
> BALTASAR GRACIÁN Y MORALES

Advocacy skills become even more crucial when dealing with customers (or regulatory bodies and bureaucrats, for that matter).

Savvy executives begin with the realization that good clients are hard to find, and harder to keep. Naive sales executives tend to regard the client as the enemy, someone to be manipulated, "worked on," and sold. Savvy executives take the long view. They blend pragmatism with morality. They know they can "sell" the client on a product once, but if it doesn't fulfill his or her promises, no one will buy it a second time.

Savvy executives see the client as an ally—someone who will likely return if the product or service is every bit as good as promised. Savvy executives know that if they make themselves invaluable to the client, they may win that client for life.

Both the naive and the savvy executive hone their presentation skills. Both realize the value of a well-turned phrase. Both know how to stroke a client. What sets savvy executives apart is that they are not merely actors reciting lines. Instead, their words and actions spring from the sobering realization that if they are to be around to serve *any* customer next year, they must serve the best interests of this client every day.

THE FOUR HUMAN QUALITIES
AN EXECUTIVE MUST POSSESS

To get along with superiors, peers, subordinates, and clients, an executive must possess and develop four crucial human qualities.

EMPATHY

The capacity to sense and share another's feelings

When I'm getting ready to reason with a man, I spend one third of my time thinking about myself and what I'm going to say—and two thirds thinking about him and what he is going to say.
BENJAMIN DISRAELI

We like to share our time and concerns with empathetic people because we sense that they truly hear and understand us—and *care*. We also want to share our ideas and experiences with them. Empathetic executives thus evoke more than mere good feelings. They also attract much *information*, thereby enhancing their effectiveness.

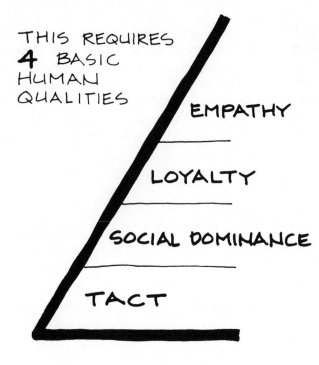

THIS REQUIRES
4 BASIC
HUMAN
QUALITIES

EMPATHY

LOYALTY

SOCIAL DOMINANCE

TACT

LOYALTY

Willingness to put the interests of others before one's own, identify with an organization, and be a member of the team

In thy face I see
The map of honor, truth,
And loyalty.
SHAKESPEARE, *HENRY VI*

The boss who gives loyalty is entitled to expect it from others. The acerbic critic Ambrose Bierce defined gratitude as the hope that someone who had just done you a favor will do so again! Loyalty might be akin to that. We give loyalty hoping to build something greater in which we may later share. Like the Three Musketeers, we embrace the notion of one for all and all for one. If we believe in the ideals of a person or an organization, then, by helping them, we can believe that we are improving the lot of Everyman, along with our own. Well-placed loyalty is thus a transforming quality. Japan's rise—and America's decline—may have a lot to do with loyalty. In Japan loyalty is a key value, whereas in America it seems to be in decline.

SOCIAL DOMINANCE

*The capacity, one way or another,
without resorting to mere authority,
to impress one's viewpoint upon
others so that they willingly accept it*

*The commander should try above
all to establish personal and
comradely contact with his men,
but without giving away an inch
of his authority.*
FIELD MARSHAL ERWIN ROMMEL

The executive who cannot dominate is disadvantaged in a leadership role. He or she may be able to overcome this disadvantage, but to do so will not be easy. An executive may dominate in many ways: by virtue of practical intelligence, by powers of empathy, by poise or grace, by reputation, by sheer physical presence, by being able to satisfy the needs of another. The socially dominant person is comfortable in virtually any social setting. Of course, the key to social dominance is to match one's style to the situation.

Harry Truman used to tell a wonderful story of taking command of a field artillery battalion, as a captain, in 1918:

> I told them I knew they had been making trouble for the previous commanders. I said: "I didn't come over here to get along with you. You've got to get along with me. And if there are any of you who can't, then speak up and I'll bust you right back." We got along.

TACT

*The faculty of saying and doing
the right thing at the right time*

Tact is after all a form of mind reading.
SARAH ORNE JEWETT

Tact is the *manifestation of judgment and empathy.* It is social intelligence in operation. It is a ready and refined sense of what is fitting and proper in dealing with others, so as to win goodwill, or, at the very least, to avoid giving offense. It is the enviable capacity of negotiating difficult situations with poise, and to the satisfaction of all parties.

The value of tact is illustrated in the oft-told story of a young priest who approached his cardinal. "Can I smoke while praying?" he asked. "Oh, no!" said the cardinal, barely looking up. "That wouldn't be right at all."

Hearing of the cardinal's response, a colleague and fellow smoker said to the first priest, "You should have been more tactful. Watch!" He then approached the cardinal. "Father, I have a troubling theological question. I like to pray as often as I can, especially during the quiet breaks of the busy day. Sometimes, when I am relaxed and enjoying my pipe, I fall into a contemplative mood and feel beset by a desire to pray. Father, is it wise for me to stifle that urging to pray at those times, or should I just go right ahead?" The cardinal answered quickly: "Go right ahead! *Never* stifle the urge to pray, my son, no matter what the circumstance."

THE FOUR CRUCIAL
COMMUNICATIONS BEHAVIORS

Be swift to hear, slow to speak.
JAMES I.19

An executive will rise or fall according to her communication skills, for at least three quarters of her time involves *communicating,* and much of the rest contemplating how to communicate most effectively.

An executive must master four fundamental communications skills.

IN ADDITION TO THE FOUR
BASIC HUMAN QUALITIES
AN EXECUTIVE MUST ALSO POSSESS

4 SPECIFIC
COMMUNICATION
SKILLS

LISTENING

DISCUSSING

WRITING

ADVOCATING

IN FACT,
EXECUTIVES SPEND
75 PERCENT OF THEIR TIME
COMMUNICATING . . .

AND MUCH OF THE REST OF THE
TIME **THINKING** ABOUT **WHAT**
TO COMMUNICATE

AND **HOW**
TO GO
ABOUT IT

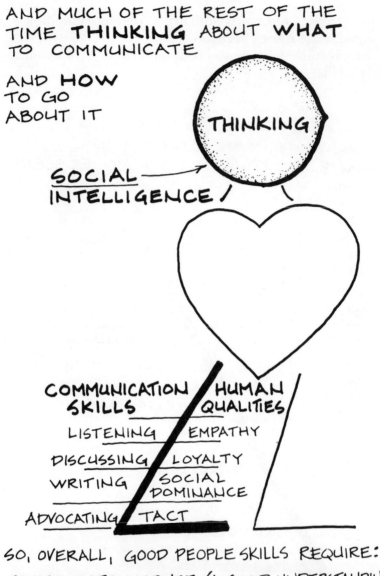

SOCIAL INTELLIGENCE

THINKING

COMMUNICATION SKILLS
LISTENING
DISCUSSING
WRITING
ADVOCATING

HUMAN QUALITIES
EMPATHY
LOYALTY
SOCIAL DOMINANCE
TACT

SO, OVERALL, GOOD PEOPLE SKILLS REQUIRE:

- **SOCIAL INTELLIGENCE** (A GOOD UNDERSTANDING OF PEOPLE AND HOW TO GET ALONG WITH THEM)

- **COMMUNICATION SKILLS:** LISTENING/ DISCUSSING / WRITING / ADVOCATING

- **HUMAN QUALITIES:** EMPATHY / LOYALTY SOCIAL DOMINANCE / TACT

LISTENING

*A man is already halfway in love
with any woman who listens to him.*
BRENDAN FRANCIS

Listening is more than remaining silent while looking attentive. Listening is making the *effort* to hear. It is paying attention. It is both hearing words and sensing meaning. It is discovering the feeling of what they're trying to convey.

Pearl Bailey said, "To talk to someone who does not listen is enough to tense the devil." We all know what she means. On the other hand, the psychologist Elton Mayo observed that "one friend, one person who truly takes the trouble to listen to us as we consider our problem, can change our whole outlook on the world."

The act of listening can change the attitude of both the listener and the speaker. And, when someone truly listens to us, then we too may come to hear what we are actually saying—and in that hearing, come to change position without the listener uttering a word.

Great executives take care to fully understand what the other person is saying; for, even if they finally choose to disagree, they want to be sure of what it is they're disagreeing with.

DISCUSSING

*Only if we can restrain ourselves is
conversation possible. Good talk
rises upon much self-discipline . . .
the unluckiest insolvent in the
world is the man whose expenditure
of speech is too great for this
income of ideas.*
CHRISTOPHER MORLEY

Discussion has two major purposes: to exchange information and to build goodwill. Virtually every dialogue provides the opportunity to pursue these worthy goals.

Discussion should be conducted more like the game of tennis than the game of golf. In golf, you go on attempting to hit your own ball; in tennis, you wait for your opponent to return your shots. Savvy executives thus treat virtually all discussions—including debates, and out-and-out arguments—as *conversations.* They are careful to listen about as often as they speak. They take care to heed the other party, even if only to collect information and intelligence.

Sometimes, of course, we want simply to discover what we think, like Alice of *Through the Looking-Glass* fame, who said, "How can I know what I think till I see what I say?" Or Oliver Wendell Holmes, who observed, "I talk half the time to find out my own thoughts, as a schoolboy turns his pockets inside out to see what is in them. One brings to light all sorts of personal properties he had forgotten in his inventory." It is entirely legitimate to do this, of course, just so long as we allow that same privilege for the other person!

WRITING

> *You don't write because you want to say something; you write because you have something to say.*
> F. SCOTT FITZGERALD

Writing *is* thinking. The writing part is easy. The thinking part is hard. People don't write badly because their vocabularies are limited, or because they can't string words together: they write unclearly because their *minds* are not clear. Either they have nothing to say or their ideas are unformed.

To know how to do something, and to know how to put that knowledge down on paper, are two different things.

Before you begin to write you must have something to say, and then bring that thought into consciousness. The typical executive finds this very difficult. Often, he simply hasn't got any thoughts to work with—he's got nothing to say. Really! In such cases he often writes simply in order to impress people. The result is frequently jargon-ridden, turgid, nonsensical prose.

The savvy executive, by contrast, marshals her thoughts and polishes them before showing them outside her office. She also understands the three keys to good corporate writing: A piece of intelligence that needs to be committed to paper (otherwise don't bother). Cogency and brevity in saying it (short memos take more time to write than long ones, but the time is well spent). And, getting the *tone* right. Each of these elements is important, of course, but for an executive getting the tone right is crucial. People will forgive us for being muddleheaded or long-winded, but they will detest us for being pompous or rude. The key to getting the tone right, in practically all correspondence, lies in addressing the reader as if he or she were sitting directly opposite you and you were having a friendly chat. The other thing, of course, is not to send an unhappy communication until mulling it overnight. And then destroying it.

ADVOCATING

> *Would you persuade, speak of interest, not of reason.*
> BENJAMIN FRANKLIN

To advocate is to attempt to make an argument in behalf of an idea or a person. The purpose of advocacy is persuasion. The advocate wants to instill an idea, or change an idea in order to bring about a change in thinking or behavior.

Advocacy is not the same as mere dominance. The cynic says: "If you've got them by their private parts, their hearts and minds will follow." The savvy executive says: "If you get them by the hearts and minds, you'll have your hands free to deal with the enemy."

To advocate is thus to reach for the heart and the mind, usually in that order. The tools of the advocate are words and tact. Thus, the executive who lacks tact is seldom going to be an effective advocate.

If you are going to be a successful advocate, keep three things in mind: First, you must link what you want to something that the other party wants. He should see that *he* will benefit by changing his mind or behavior. If he doesn't see that, then you'll probably lose your case. Second, you must play to the heart rather than the mind. You can *pretend* to play to the mind, of course, but ultimately it is the heart that has to be won. Get the heart, and the mind will surely follow. And, third, you must usually be prepared to persevere. I know from first-hand experience that perseverance can sometimes succeed, even when all else fails:

> I once applied to a bank for a loan to buy a house—and was turned down. It was a nice house, and I needed a big loan. By means of some Machiavellian maneuvers I got myself in to see the manager of the bank to restate my case. He listened to all my arguments very politely. Then he too said no, and he stood up, indicating that the interview was over. I needed that money, however. I had to settle, and I had no other source of funds. Remaining seated, I looked him in the eye and said, "Maybe we could just go through it again." Then I leaned back in my chair to show I wasn't leaving. "Oh, all right then we'll give you the loan!" he said, exasperated.

BEHAVIORAL CHECKLIST #2

Specific People Behaviors
Demonstrated by Successful Executives

A. *Communicating.* Leaders and managers spend most of their time communicating. Key communications behaviors include:

1. *Sound verbal communication skills.* Is accurate, organized, articulate, concise.
2. *Developed listening skills.* Encourages a steady flow of information from subordinates. Hears and heeds good advice.
3. *Appropriate writing skills.* Memos, letters, reports are organized, cogent, concise, attuned to recipient's viewpoint.
4. *Subtle influencing, nudging skills.* An advocate rather than an autocrat.

B. *Leading.* Leadership might be defined as the art and science of building, maintaining, and influencing others in the pursuit of greater goals than they themselves might have believed possible. Specific leadership behaviors include

1. *Presses for results.* Sets high but realistic goals, and communicates tenable expectations. Applies appropriate pressure. Assertive as necessary.
2. *Paints the big picture for subordinates.* Shows the organization's annual goals, general strategies, and explains how the local unit fits in and contributes.
3. *Leads or facilitates development of the local unit's objectives and strategies.* Ensures these are consistent with the broader goals of the organization.
4. *Delegates effectively.* Designates responsibility and authority for achieving objectives and lets go.
5. *Monitors expeditiously.* Holds regular one-on-one meetings with subordinates, gives informal performance feedback, disciplines tactfully. Is neither nitpicking of details nor abandoning in style.
6. *Fosters development.* Attuned to subordinates' feelings. Helps subordinates to grow. Provides positive reinforcement. Available.
7. *Forges trust.* Establishes "adult-to-adult" relationships.

Projects "I-trust-you attitude." Keeps promises, represents subordinates fairly to senior management.

8. *Fosters team spirit.* Encourages cooperation and exchange of ideas, gives credit for contributions.
9. *Welcomes innovation from subordinates.* Encourages subordinates to develop routines, methods, and systems permitting efficient unit operations.
10. *Conducts effective meetings.* Encourages involvement without losing control, gets participation while allowing dissent.
11. *Eases conflicts.* Resolves differences between individuals or subordinate units without showing favoritism.
12. *Recruits and retains strong subordinates:* not just people willing to conform.

C. *Nurturing.* A leader devotes time and energy to nurturing relationships with the many people upon whom he or she necessarily depends to help achieve his/her goals. Specific nurturing behaviors include

1. *Keeps the links and channels open.* Is a communications conduit rather than a barrier. Passes timely, relevant information to:
   Superiors—gives both the good news and the bad;
   Peers—fosters information sharing;
   Subordinates—keeps them informed and involved.
2. *Relates appropriately with superiors.* Represents self and department confidently and positively. Neither overly assertive, deferent, nor political.
3. *Fosters team spirit with peers.* Shares ideas and information. Advocates and influences but is not overly political or manipulative.
4. *Shares credit.* Gives recognition to deserving peers and appropriate peer subordinates.
5. *Fosters overall team spirit.* Encourages cooperation of subordinates with subordinates of management peers in other units.
6. *Protects subordinates.* Ensures subordinates are not pushed around or unfairly used by others.
7. *Marshals resources.* Gets people, budget, equipment, wherewithal needed to achieve department's objective.
8. *Maintains community standing.* Professional and effective in external relationships—with vendors, customers, government officials.

ELEMENT #8
ADJUSTMENT

He won't get to the root of his
problem, because the root of his
problem is himself.
CARROLL O'CONNOR ON ARCHIE BUNKER

Coward: a person who in an
emergency thinks with his legs.
AMBROSE BIERCE

Napoleon said "The first quality of a commander-in-chief is a cool head to receive a correct impression of things." A cool head is the head of a mature adult. It is a head that is mature, adjusted, and well balanced.

Great executives virtually always have their heads on straight. They see the world clearly, go after what they want, and, along the way, make appropriate adjustments to their goals, strategies, and behavior.

Mediocre executives, on the other hand, are usually impaired by underlying immaturity that compels them to embark upon unwise ventures, attempt to live in fantasy worlds, fail to deal with pressure rationally, and blame others when things go wrong.

In reality, cool, well-balanced heads are not easy to find. An important study conducted by the psychologist Leo Scrole in New York during the sixties—and borne out in similar surveys since—revealed that

- Only 18.5 percent of people are well adjusted and free from mental illness.
- 58.5 percent showed mild to moderate mental-health problems.
- 23.5 percent showed marked to severe problems.

As a quick rule of thumb, then, we can safely say that emotional immaturity is the *norm,* for more than three quarters of the population fail to grow into well-balanced, conscious, rational, autonomous adults.

WELL ADJUSTED EXECUTIVES
HAVE THEIR HEADS ON STRAIGHT

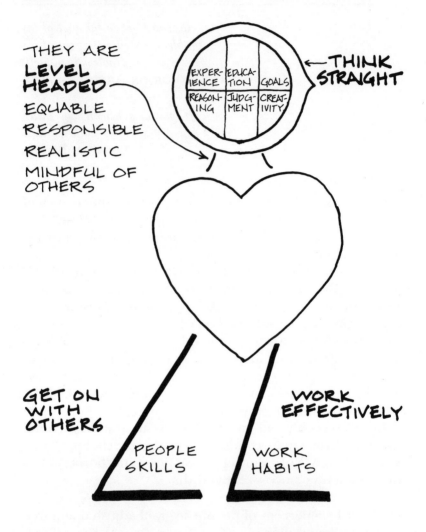

THEY ARE
LEVEL HEADED
EQUABLE
RESPONSIBLE
REALISTIC
MINDFUL OF OTHERS

← THINK STRAIGHT

EXPER-IENCE	EDUCA-TION	GOALS
REASON-ING	JUDG-MENT	CREAT-IVITY

GET ON WITH OTHERS

PEOPLE SKILLS

WORK EFFECTIVELY

WORK HABITS

THEY ARE MATURE AND FREE OF
COUNTERPRODUCTIVE NEUROSES

For the most part, emotional maladjustment springs from an unhappy emotional climate in the home, and poor parenting. A responsible, thoughtful parent ideally sees his or her role as being to raise a happy, self-reliant adult. Unfortunately, for many reasons, this seldom happens. Among the myriad of things that can go wrong, some children are abandoned, beaten, or rejected. Many others are overly cosseted or indulged, an altogether more subtle form of abuse. Any such experiences will affect the developing child, and ultimately the fully grown adult.

It is easy to see that the child who is openly abused may grow into a hostile adult. Less obvious, however, is the damage that occurs where a child is raised, as happens in many middle-class homes, in a situation where the parents *seem* to provide a loving happy climate, yet, in reality, in many covert ways abuse and reject the child. This often happens where parents stay together either "to keep up appearances" or "for the good of the children." In fact, such parents frequently resent and blame the children for all kinds of problems, including the state of the marriage. And, of course, the children grow up in an emotional never-never land, where something is always wrong, and undercurrents and tensions constitute the order of daily life, yet the child cannot rationally determine the cause of the problem. The emotional growth of such children is often stunted ultimately producing neurotic adults plagued by anxieties, suspicions, and resentments.

Similar problems occur where children are pampered and cosseted, for they too often become emotionally crippled, and rendered unable to function as self-reliant adults. Such children survive childhood by adopting various defense mechanisms, including emotional withdrawal and emotional manipulation. Unfortunately, these coping devices become ingrained, and form a part of the mental baggage that the child carries into adult life.

Quite apart from problems at home, other social factors also conspire to hamper emotional growth, including:

Over-Lengthy Education. In some circles it is believed that a person is not suitably educated to take employment until he or she has completed not one but two university degrees. Thus, the perceived need for continuing education involves many people not becoming financially or emotionally independent until into their middle and late twenties.

The Drug Syndrome.   Drugs have become a more or less universal means of denying reality. No emotional growth takes place when a person is under the influence of drugs.

Yuppie Values.   Recently minted MBAs often command big bucks simply for brokering transactions. Their concerns are for themselves, and the often transient relationships in which they become engaged. The capacity to remain absorbed in this kind of world can contribute to a lack of real emotional growth, and consequent immaturity.

THE TWO MAJOR MANIFESTATIONS OF IMMATURITY

Emotional immaturity manifests itself in two major ways:

- Overdependency, in which the sufferer never succeeds in passive, submissive, symbiotic relationships with parental surrogates.
- An incapacity to outgrow and control infantile drives and impulses.

Let's examine each of these problems.

MANIFESTATION #1:
EMOTIONAL OVERDEPENDENCY

For convenience sake, immature people may be ranked on a continuum, ranging from conformist through manipulative. Let's look at each end of the spectrum.

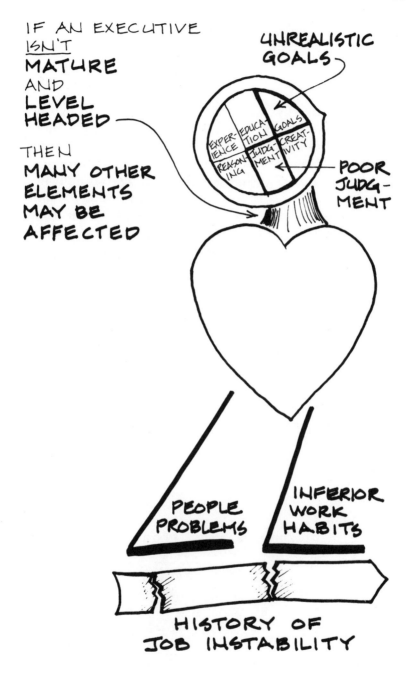

IF AN EXECUTIVE
ISN'T
MATURE
AND
LEVEL
HEADED

THEN
MANY OTHER
ELEMENTS
MAY BE
AFFECTED

UNREALISTIC
GOALS

EXPER-IENCE · EDUCA-TION · GOALS
REASON-ING · JUDG-MENT · CREAT-IVITY

POOR
JUDG-
MENT

PEOPLE
PROBLEMS

INFERIOR
WORK
HABITS

HISTORY OF
JOB INSTABILITY

THE CONFORMIST

> *You can't be wise when you are afraid.*
> ERIC LINKLATER

The conformist was taught to *obey*. He was told that the world was a treacherous place, but that everything might be okay if he would only follow the instructions of his parents, his schoolteachers, his government, and God. He was told that he would be rewarded for conforming, but punished for the unspeakable crime of attempting to think for himself. In consequence, in later life, although he can show great academic attainment and make a sober, conservative appearance, it will become apparent soon enough that

- his judgment is very poor. Though he is often highly educated, and can reason in a straight line, he nonetheless seems to lack a mind of his own. If he can't find the solution to a problem in a company manual or a business text, then for him it simply doesn't exist;
- the need to make decisions evokes great stress in him. He is a deeply worried person, fearful of being blamed or punished for doing the wrong thing, or, indeed, *anything* at all;
- even when he is simply following orders, he still seems to have a knack for tripping himself up and getting things wrong.

THE MANIPULATOR

> *Scoundrels are always sociable.*
> ARTHUR SCHOPENHAUER

> *Every one fault seeming monstrous,*
> *till his fellow fault came to match it.*
> SHAKESPEARE, *AS YOU LIKE IT*

The manipulator learned early in life to manipulate those with whom she came in contact by a skillful blend of charm, tears, and rage. Because she was indulged, she failed to mature; in consequence, in later life, although she will probably make a fine, charming first impression, it will soon enough become apparent that:

- her judgment is very poor. She continues to see the world through the prism of a child, and is thus prone to wishful or delusional thinking;
- she suffers a sense of *entitlement.* She feels she should be looked after, and that someone ought to be attending to this on a regular basis;
- when, as happens fairly frequently, she gets into trouble, she expects others to come to her rescue;
- she perceives herself as a *victim,* and is quick to blame others for the things that go wrong in her life;
- she shows a remarkable inability to learn from past errors;
- she finds it difficult to contain her anger, and can fly into tears or rages quickly;
- she is incredibly *selfish,* self-absorbed, and narcissistic. She shows little concern for the interests or feelings of others. She expects other people to make the effort to get on with her.

It must be borne in mind that immaturity affects virtually *all* behavior. Thus, immature people at either end of the spectrum suffer problems in fixing realistic goals, as well as moving toward them.

MANIFESTATION #2:
INCAPACITY TO OUTGROW EIGHT KEY INFANTILE DRIVES AND IMPULSES

1. SELFISHNESS

"Me, me, what's in it for me?"
The child is concerned with its own needs to the exclusion of others. The selfish adult remains absorbed in his or her own needs and interests. She does not share, and is

unhappy if she does not receive the lion's share of any pie, for she feels that this is her *entitlement*. Deposed hotel "Queen" Leona Helmsley provides one of the more interesting recent examples of such behavior.

2. IRRESPONSIBILITY

"None of this is my responsibility!"

A child, fearful of accepting responsibility for mistakes, seeks to avoid taking on adult responsibilities and hastily blames others when things go wrong. The immature adult evidences this trait in a more sophisticated fashion, offering apparently well-reasoned excuses and plausible alibis to paper over his failures. I remember dealing with a self-styled movie tycoon who acquired an important film company, raised a lot of public money, surrounded himself with a lot of incompetent sycophants—including, incredibly, a script reader who truly was functionally illiterate—and proceeded to produce some woefully unprofitable feature movies. When the company went broke, which didn't take long at all, the explanations came thick and fast: the economic climate was wrong, the critics were unfair, the movie theaters were crooked. But the tycoon was still a genius. Of course!

3. DISREGARD FOR CONSEQUENCES

"The devil made me do it!"

The child does not curb her impulses, because she cannot see very far ahead. She may also come to discover that indulgent parents will shield her from any untoward consequences. In later life such children become impulsive "adults" who rely on friends, relations, and employers to pick up the pieces. Alan Bond, Australia's most boisterous property developer, and winner of the America's Cup, illustrates the problem. Mr. Bond won international attention by purchasing Van Gogh's *Sunflowers* for a record price. People assumed, as Mr. Bond intended them to, that he must be a very rich man. In fact, he was close to broke, and it ultimately came to light that virtually none of his business activities had ever turned a profit. He simply borrowed, and borrowed, and borrowed—until the house came tumbling down!

4. PLEASURE-MINDEDNESS

"Let's play!"

Children like to pursue pleasure and play. An important part of maturing, however, lies in learning to forgo immediate pleasure in order to meet the demands of reality—such as earning money to help pay one's way. Unfortunately, many individuals never manage to strike a proper balance between the pursuit of pleasure and the demands of reality. Thus, indications of overconcern with partying, and playing, are usually a clear index of immaturity. *Playboy* founder Hugh Hefner spun such a quirk into an entire industry. Malcolm Forbes, the late publisher of *Forbes* magazine, though he gaily courted a different audience, showed a similar hedonistic bent.

5. WISHFUL THINKING

"I have a tremendous belief in myself."

Children live in a world of fairy tales, make-believe, and magic. Indulgent parents often anticipate the child's every need, thereby engendering feelings of omnipotence. Similarly, the immature adult often lives in a fantasy world divorced from reality. The wonderful British film classic *Billy Liar* is all about such an individual. Such a person believes that if he wishes for a thing with sufficient vigor, he will get it. Any tendency toward wishful thinking needs to be looked at very closely, for it is usually a harbinger of very poor judgment—no matter how intellectually gifted the sufferer. Wishful thinking is often the hallmark of such infantile business personalities as failed auto magnate John DeLorean, who proudly—and very aptly—referred to himself as a "Dream-maker."

6. NARCISSISM AND EXHIBITION

"Look at me! Look at me!"

At some time or another, the child is usually the center of attention—and certain people want this happy state to endure forever, to which end they engage in all sorts of attention-getting strategies, some subtle, some not so subtle. Such people are attracted to roles that place them in the spotlight. Public speakers, actors, televangelists often fall into this category, as do entrepreneurs who insert themselves into their television advertising campaigns. Flamboyant, publicity-seeking Victor Kiam, the man who liked the Remington razor so much that he bought the company, provides a case in point.

7. LACK OF SELF-DISCIPLINE

"I demand to make my feelings known."

Every infant is almost entirely lacking in self-control. She often discovers that crying out for a thing, or throwing a temper tantrum, will bring her parents running with whatever she wants. This soon becomes an ingrained habit that the adult herself is unable to cure, *even though she might like to do so.*

A former airline executive I worked with displayed an abundance of this trait, and was unable to restrain himself from mounting a frontal, fistal, physical attack on his successor in office—a much heftier fellow, by the way, who handled the situation with great aplomb by pulling his ferocious foe into a clutch and murmuring, "Before this gets serious, I should perhaps mention that I lead the wrestling team at college." Even where an ill-disciplined person manages to control her outbursts, she may suffer other related problems: she may be unable to evaluate her own behavior objectively, and she may suffer great difficulty in accepting constructive criticism.

8. DESTRUCTIVE TENDENCIES

"Let's have a little fun at his expense."

The urge to destroy is part of humankind that we prefer to overlook. I well remember a boy at school who had captured a live dragonfly. "I suppose you'll pull its legs off now," said a teacher who happened to be passing. "No, Sir. Wings first!" came the reply. Many adults have difficulty in checking their underlying aggressions, and seek to sublimate such urges by becoming butchers, soldiers, law-enforcement officers. Such people often enter business, too, of course, and channel their energies into the pursuit of profit. Former Yankee owner George Steinbrenner, famous for firing virtually every manager he ever hired, provides a good example of the genre. These individuals often make great salespeople, but they seldom make good managers, for their destructive urges bring them into conflict with authority, and their sadistic impulses lead them to seek scapegoats and whipping boys among their subordinates.

WHAT IT MEANS TO HAVE ONE'S HEAD ON STRAIGHT

He is happy whose circumstances suit his temper; but he is more excellent who can suit his temper to any circumstance.
DAVID HUME

However good you may be you have faults; however dull you may be you can find out what some of them are, and however slight they may be you had better make some—not too painful but patient—efforts to get rid of them.
JOHN RUSKIN

The well-adjusted person who learns to take care of herself as she grows to adulthood routinely displays the following behaviors:

- Accepts responsibility for her own behavior. Learns from failure. Does not repeat past errors.
- Is pleased to receive constructive criticism, is sincerely glad of the opportunity to improve.
- Doesn't expect special treatment.
- Meets emergencies with poise.

- Sees the world in shades of gray rather than simple black and white. Realizes that no person or situation is wholly bad or good.
- Is not impatient with reasonable delays. Realizes that the world runs to its own pace. Expects to have to make reasonable compromises.
- Wins without gloating. Endures defeat and disappointment with equanimity. Tries to learn from every loss.
- Harbors no jealousy. Is sincerely pleased for others when they enjoy success or good fortune.
- Is considerate of the opinions and feelings of others. Is a careful listener. Doesn't become defensive, closed-minded, or unduly argumentative when discussing her opinions.
- Plans for the future, rather than trusting to the inspiration of the moment.

ELEMENT # 9

OVERALL PERSONALITY STYLE

It is most true, stylus virum
arguit, *our style betrays us.*
ROBERT BURTON (1577–1640)

The style is the man himself.
GEORGES-LOUIS LECLERC DE BUFFON

Executives have an overall style that affects the way they think, the goals they choose, and the patterns of behavior they adopt.

Styles may be divided into three basic types: Dominant, Detached, and Dependent (M's, T's, and P's).

These styles have been separately identified by psychologists conducting independent research into the respective areas of goals, emotional outlook, and birth order, or place in the family.

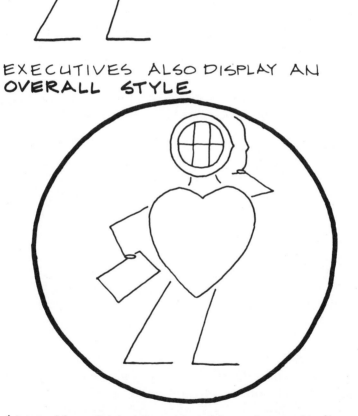

QUITE APART FROM THE INDIVIDUAL ELEMENTS THAT COMPRISE THE EXECUTIVE PSYCHE

EXECUTIVES ALSO DISPLAY AN **OVERALL STYLE**

AND ALL THE ELEMENTS OF BEHAVIOR **MAKE** THE **MOST SENSE WHEN** WE CAN **IDENTIFY THAT STYLE**

GOALS The psychologist David McLelland found that executives could be accurately classified according to three major motivational groupings: Power, Achievement, and Affiliation. Under our classification, the Power Seeker would be an M, the Achiever a T, and the Affiliator a P.

EMOTIONAL OUTLOOK Eric Berne in his wonderful book *Games People Play* postulated three major *ego states:* Parent, Adult, and Child. He observed that although a person might be able to move among these three ego states, he or she nonetheless tended to gravitate to one of the three.

- In the Parent mode, a person's attitude was dominating and dictatorial: an M.
- In the Adult mode, he/she was detached and rational: a T.
- In the Child mode, he/she was fun-loving and playful and, possibly, weak, petulant, and demanding: a P.

BIRTH ORDER Birth-order psychology tells us that a person is naturally conditioned to maintain his or her place in the family—and continue to earn the respect and attention of other family members—then, later, of the larger world. So, as a simple rule of thumb,

- The first born strives to remain dominant.
- The middle child becomes the detached mediator.
- The youngest child becomes emotionally dependent upon the parents and older siblings.

It is worth keeping in mind, however, that one's overall style will be influenced by the style of one's parents—and *their* respective places in the family. Thus, the first-born child of first-born parents will probably develop differently from the first-born child of youngest parents. Just the same, birth order is usually a crucial factor in determining personality and goals. Now let's consider each of the three basic styles a little further.

STYLES MAY BE DIVIDED INTO
THREE BASIC TYPES:

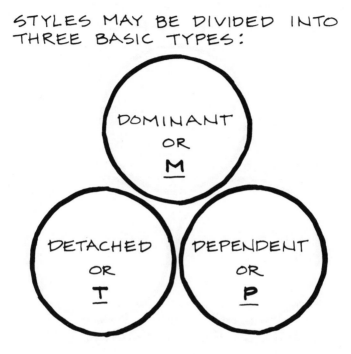

THESE PERSONALITY TRAITS DEVELOP
EARLY IN LIFE AND ARE TYPICALLY
AFFECTED BY THE INDIVIDUAL'S
PLACE IN THE FAMILY

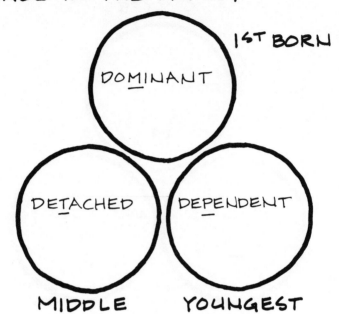

AS A ROUGH RULE OF THUMB, WE
STRIVE TO MAINTAIN ONE PECKING
ORDER:

1ST BORN – DOMINANT

MIDDLE CHILD – DETACHED

YOUNGEST CHILD – DEPENDENT

PROFILES OF THE THREE BASIC TYPES

DOMINANT (M)   The M is often the first-born child. M's central life interest is to retain and advance his or her ascendancy. His/Her prime motivations are power, and status. Achievement may also serve to secure and advance his/her dominance.

M's usually present themselves as leaders. They are attracted to management roles, and usually lead by virtue of presence and assertiveness. M's management style is likely to be autocratic. M's office and home are usually at good addresses, and may be decorated with photos of M receiving prizes or awards. M's underlying fear is loss of power and status.

Chrysler chief executive Lee Iacocca is probably an M.

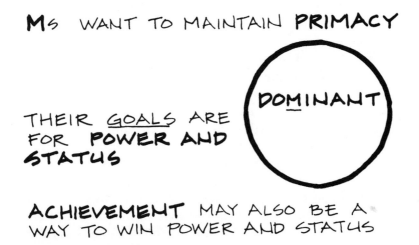

Ms WANT TO MAINTAIN **PRIMACY**

THEIR <u>GOALS</u> ARE FOR **POWER AND STATUS**

DOMINANT

ACHIEVEMENT MAY ALSO BE A WAY TO WIN POWER AND STATUS

M's MAJOR UNDERLYING FEAR IS THE **FEAR OF FAILURE**

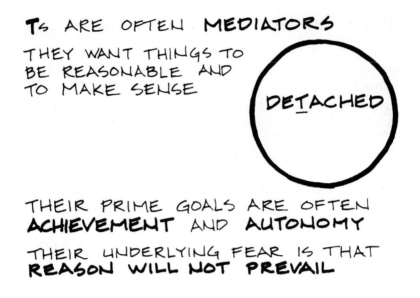

Ts ARE OFTEN **MEDIATORS**

THEY WANT THINGS TO
BE REASONABLE AND
TO MAKE SENSE

DETACHED

THEIR PRIME GOALS ARE OFTEN
ACHIEVEMENT AND **AUTONOMY**

THEIR UNDERLYING FEAR IS THAT
REASON WILL NOT PREVAIL

DETACHED (T) The Detached person is often a middle child, or the offspring of one. T's prize reason and logic, for without it, they would probably be run over by the M's and outcharmed by the P's. The T's central life interest is to make sense of the world and his/her place in it. They often show needs for realistic achievement and autonomy.

Detached people usually present themselves as calm, rational types. They order their lives carefully. They may work in an austere hi-tech setting. They probably know how to use their personal computers. Their homes are likely to be very functional, and to reflect good sense, good taste, and good value. They are team players, who gravitate to the mediator's role. When called upon to lead, their rationality and sense of fair play command considerable respect. They are often more comfortable playing a supporting role, however. Their management style is likely to be rational and democratic. Their underlying fear is that reason may not prevail. Former U.S. presidential advisor Zbigniew Brzezinski is probably a T.

Ps ARE USUALLY ACCUSTOMED TO
GIVING AND GETTING **AFFECTION**

THEIR NEEDS
ARE FOR
AFFILIATION,
ACCEPTANCE, AND
APPROVAL

DEPENDENT

THEIR UNDERLYING FEAR IS
REJECTION

DEPENDENT (P) Emotionally dependent people are often youngest children, whose central life interest is to win and hold the affection of those about them. They are affiliators who belong to many clubs and service organizations, and need to feel the warmth, companionship, and emotional support of other people. They like to serve others, thereby winning their approval, acceptance, and love. They are not necessarily overdependent, but frequently tend in that direction.

Dependent people usually present themselves as warmhearted. They may be somewhat careless in their work habits. They are attracted to sales, human resources, and public relations roles. If elected to leadership roles—which is far more likely to happen in a social than a work setting—their style is likely to be *laissez-faire.* Their offices and homes often bear photos of their parents, spouse, children, and pets. Their underlying fears are of rejection or disapproval. Many outstanding salespeople are P's.

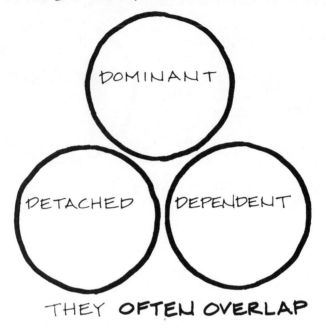

THESE THREE STYLES ARE **NOT DISCRETE**, OR SELF-CONTAINED

THEY **OFTEN OVERLAP**

THE THREE MAJOR SUBTYPES— AND SIX MORE SUB-SUB-TYPES

The three types are seldom entirely self-contained. So, it is very useful to think of the circles in our model as overlapping, thereby creating three more styles. We might also choose to weigh each of these three styles, thereby creating six more styles. Thus:

The Dominant Dependent (MP)—plus, Mp, and mP.
The Dominant Detached (MT)—plus Mt and mT.
The Detached Dependent (TP)—plus Tp and tP.

THE DOMINANT DEPENDENT (MP) The MP wants to be seen to be powerful, successful, and strong, in order to deny and compensate for fairly acute emotional dependen-

THE OVERLAP CREATES AT LEAST
4 MORE CATEGORIES OF STYLE

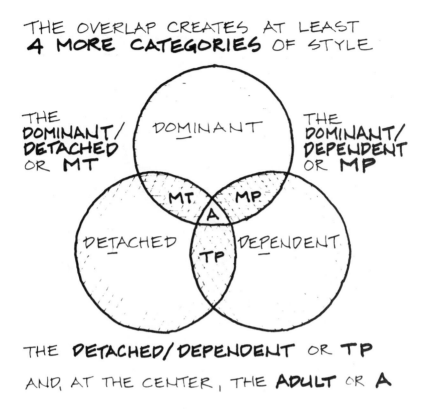

THE
DOMINANT/
DETACHED
OR **MT**

THE
DOMINANT/
DEPENDENT
OR **MP**

THE **DETACHED/DEPENDENT** OR **TP**

AND, AT THE CENTER, THE **ADULT** OR **A**

cies that usually stem from an indulged childhood. MP's show strong needs for status and visibility, often going so far as to hire public relations firms to place articles extolling imagined achievements. MP's often seem to succeed in business, but, in reality, the success is usually overrated and comes at considerable emotional cost to the MP—a cost so great that MP's often unconsciously seek ways to sabotage their own goals.

MP's usually present themselves as people of great charm, or of great aggression—or both. MP's are often sales "stars" who become promoted to management, only to fail. The MP suffers difficulty in concealing his or her emotional dependencies, which are generally evidenced by manipulation and charm, followed by further manipulation

MPs (A VERY COMMON STYLE)
OFTEN GET **CAUGHT IN A BIND**

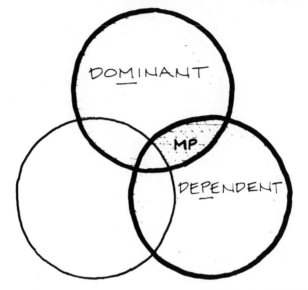

FOR THEY WANT <u>BOTH</u> THE **STATUS**
OF A LEADERSHIP ROLE <u>AND</u> THE
AFFECTION OF THOSE WHOM THEY
SEEK TO DIRECT — AND **THIS IS
NOT ALWAYS POSSIBLE**

and anger. One of the better known MP's would probably be real estate "magnate" Donald Trump.

THE DOMINANT DETACHED (MT) The MT, perhaps the first-born child of second-born parents, usually aspires to lead. Though often somewhat socially restrained, MT's will diligently and intelligently apply themselves to this goal. MT's prize intellect and knowledge as a means of getting ahead, and are likely to pursue and possess master's degrees in business. An MT's style is usually pragmatic. MT's are team players, with an open mind and a keen receptiveness to innovation and change. They approach business as if it were a game of chess, and strive to come up with the

MTs ARE USUALLY
FAIRLY COOL LEADERS WHO
DOMINATE BY VIRTUE OF **INTELLECT**
RATHER THAN MERE ~~EBULLIENCE~~

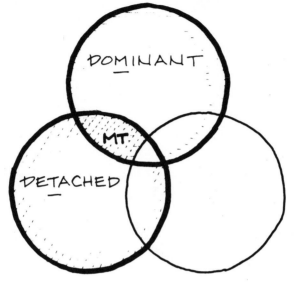

best strategy and moves. MT's probably include current U.S. President George Bush and fallen Wall Street operator Michael Milken, who led the now defunct firm of Drexel, Burnham, Lambert to the stars—and back again!

THE DETACHED DEPENDENT (TP)   The TP, perhaps the youngest child of second-born parents, is more likely to be a staff executive than a line executive. TP's turn their strong intellects to winning the approval and acceptance of others in a supporting role. TP's are likely to be fairly introverted, "lonely loners," who have trouble attracting or holding much of a following. TP's often gravitate to backroom roles in strategic planning, or purchasing. TP's

TPs (AN INFREQUENT EXECUTIVE STYLE)
ARE LIKELY TO BE **LOW KEY** PEOPLE,
TYPICALLY UNINTERESTED IN ASSUMING
LINE LEADERSHIP ROLES

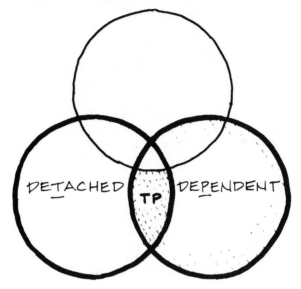

might include former U.S. President Jimmy Carter and close aide to the Reagan administration Robert McFarlane, who attempted suicide rather than face cross-examination during the congressional Iran-Contra hearings.

THE ADULT IN THE CENTER   At the center of our model we have a style that embodies all of the above qualities. This is the style of the truly well-adjusted Adult, who matches his style to the demands of the situation in which he finds himself. Such individuals are sometimes altogether too well adjusted to aspire to leadership roles, but can make excellent advisors and stand-ins.

As — TRULY ADULT EXECUTIVES
ARE AT THE **CENTER** OF THE MODEL

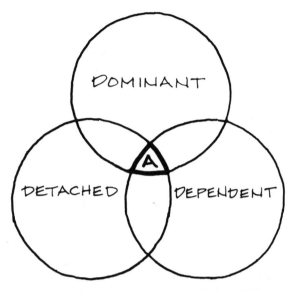

THEY ARE USUALLY **PRAGMATISTS**
WHO RESPOND TO EACH SITUATION
WITH **NO OVERRIDING PERSONALITY
STYLE**

ELEMENT # 10

STAGE IN LIFE—AND
GENERAL DIRECTION

> *The old man who observes two or*
> *three generations is like one who*
> *sits in the conjuror's booth at a*
> *fair, and sees the tricks two or*
> *three times. They are meant to be*
> *seen only once.*
> ARTHUR SCHOPENHAUER.

Since success in life is determined by fulfillment of the
psychic contract, it is important to identify a person's stage
in life in the journey through time toward winning or los-

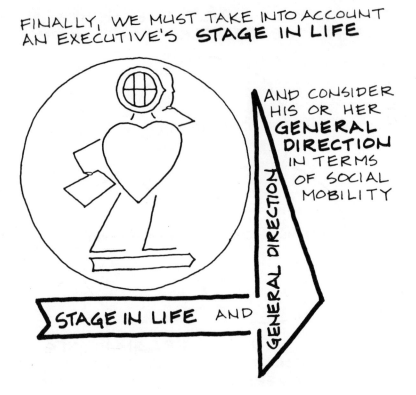

FINALLY, WE MUST TAKE INTO ACCOUNT AN EXECUTIVE'S **STAGE IN LIFE**

AND CONSIDER HIS OR HER **GENERAL DIRECTION** IN TERMS OF SOCIAL MOBILITY

STAGE IN LIFE AND GENERAL DIRECTION

ing, and beyond. This not easy to do, for while grasping the concept of life stages seems a simple matter, we cannot truly know what a particular stage might entail until we experience it for ourselves. As the French philosopher Amiel noted:

> To understand things one must first have been in them, and then have come out of them; so that first there must be captivity and then deliverance, illusion followed by disillusion, enthusiasm by disappointment. He who is still under the spell, and he who has never felt the spell, are equally incompetent. We only know well what we have first believed, then judged. To understand we must be free, yet not always have been free.

Let's now consider a fairly typical life itinerary, comprising ten or so overlapping stages.

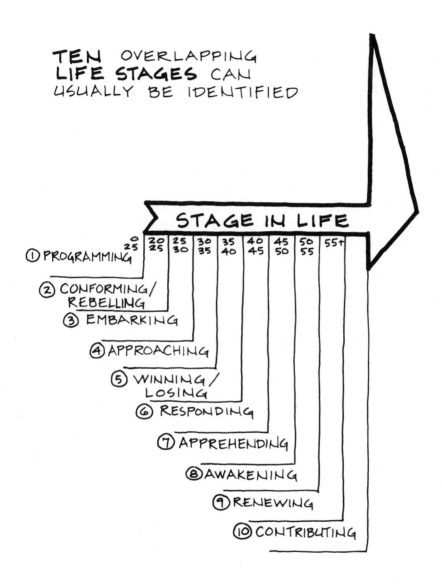

TEN OVERLAPPING
LIFE STAGES CAN
USUALLY BE IDENTIFIED

STAGE IN LIFE

	0 25	20 25	25 30	30 35	35 40	40 45	45 50	50 55	55+
① PROGRAMMING									
② CONFORMING/ REBELLING									
③ EMBARKING									
④ APPROACHING									
⑤ WINNING/ LOSING									
⑥ RESPONDING									
⑦ APPREHENDING									
⑧ AWAKENING									
⑨ RENEWING									
⑩ CONTRIBUTING									

Stage 1. To Age 18: Programming. The child is inculcated with a value system, attitudes, opinions, a range of emotions, an outlook on life, and, of course, a psychic contract containing the ultimate goals that spell success or failure. The lifestyle expectation in the psychic contract will largely determine the extent of any social goals, and general direction, and the core values will crucially affect capacity to befriend and rise among persons of higher social status.

Stage 2. Ages 18–25: Conforming or Rebelling. The challenge of moving from childhood to adulthood is to become an individual, while still remaining part of the community. Thus the eternal dilemma of youth: how to rebel and conform at the same time? The apparent conundrum is usually resolved fairly neatly, however, by defying one's parents and copying one's peers, especially as they tune into the rebellious anti-heroes of the generation: for some it was Frank Sinatra or Elvis Presley, for others it was the Beatles or the Rolling Stones, more recently it has been Talking Heads and Galaxie 500.

This stage in life is reflected in the Parable of the Prodigal Son, who defies his stern, religious father by leaving home and devoting his life to the pursuit of earthly pleasures. After experiencing the hard ways of the world, however, the son repents his profligacy and returns home, presumably to set about making good on a psychic contract calling for him to become his father's clone.

Stage 3. Ages 25–30: Embarking. Now, guided by the prime parental directive, the young adult "sets out to make a mark on the world" by becoming established in the kind of career that hopefully will permit the fulfillment of his or her lifestyle expectations.

The embarker is usually intelligent and well educated but, through lack of exposure, seldom mature or well rounded. Conformist embarkers are often anxious and willing to learn from their superiors, whom they often come to regard as heroes, leading the devoted embarker toward enlightenment, and a place in the sun.

Other embarkers want to learn but don't like to be taught, and manifest many of the negative traits of our old friend the Dominant Dependent, or MP. They oscillate between certitude and insecurity, asserting opinions with great rigidity, yet suffering tremendous self-doubt. They demand to be taken seriously, yet there are great gaps of knowledge and understanding, which are masked by uncompromising declarations.

Stage 4. Ages 30–37: Approaching.

Now the executive is more experienced and, with any luck, this has brought a measure of maturity and confidence. The former conformist may now be able to work without the need for rules and guidance. And the rebel may now be able to admit to feelings of uncertainty in the face of ambiguous situations—and therefore be better equipped to deal with such situations.

The embarker begins to appreciate what must be done in order to fulfill the psychic contract, and soon enough, he or she will see those goals coming into sight, or receding. Now we say that the embarker is "about to make his mark on the world"—an expression that Sigmund Freud felt was clearly related to early toilet training, by the way. (So too, he felt, were such expressions as "made his pile," "filthy lucre," "rolling in the stuff," and so on.)

Stage 5. Ages 35–45: Winning/Losing.

To win or lose is to make good—or fail to make good—on the psychic contract, by fulfilling the prime parental objective, following the guiding criteria for success, meeting the lifestyle expectation, and, finally, realizing the culminating achievement.

This is usually the time in life when financial needs press hardest. It is a time for paying heavy bills on house, spouse, children, cars—"the full catastrophe," in the felicitous words of Zorba the Greek.

Stage 6. Ages 39–47: Responding.

The initial response to both winning and losing is *burnout.*

- The winner is likely to empathize with the Peggy Lee standard, "Is that all there is?" She feels empty and burned out, because the goals that pulled her along are now gone, leaving her without immediate purpose or direction, appreciative of the wonderings of Joseph Heller's midlife character Bob Slocum in *Something Happened*. "How did I get here? Somebody pushed me. Somebody set me off in this direction, and other hands must have touched themselves to the controls at various times, for I would not have picked this way for the world."

- The loser suffers a sense of disgrace, from which she might like to flee, like the man who for twenty years began his commute to work by making a left turn out of Oak Street, until one day he began to contemplate another way out:

> To turn right, or to turn left at Oak Street,
> That's the choice I face every day,
> And I don't know which takes more courage,
> The staying or the running away.

A second category of loser may also be postulated: the *At-Leaster*—the person who didn't quite win, but who didn't quite lose either. The personality of the At-Leaster often reflects the dictum, "Cynicism is the last refuge of the idealist," for At-Leasters usually display an ironical—and somewhat envying—sense of seen-it-all sadness. At-Leasters say:

- "I didn't get to be chief executive, but at least they gave me a corner office and a nice title."
- "I didn't get a book published, but at least I got these very nice rejection letters."
- "I may not have saved the world, but at least I'm helping to preserve the environment by sorting my garbage into recyclable bundles."

At such a time, no matter what the outcome of the psychic contract, winners and losers will often seek an entirely new lifestyle and switch career, spouse, friends, car, and whatever. This knee-jerk response usually fails to quench inner demons, however.

Stage 7. Ages 45–55: Apprehending.   In our twenties, we speculate about death with great intensity but know that we will live forever. Normally it is not until fifty or so that we actually catch sight of the dark at the end of the our own tunnel—a vision usually brought into view by the remorseless aging of a parent, the marriage of a child, or perhaps the accidental death of a peer. Now, we apprehend our own mortality. Now, we truly know that life is brief, and becoming briefer.

Often, the stage of apprehending overlaps the stage of winning and responding, leading to a full-blown "midlife crisis," wherein the sufferer is overcome with melancholy and depression, and left grieving for years wasted and powers lost. Now we understand the lament of the mother in Eugene O'Neill's *Long Day's Journey into Night:*

> *. . . None of us can help the things life has done to us. They're done before you realize it, and once they're done they make you do other things until at last everything comes between you and what you'd like to be, and you've lost your true self forever.*

Stage 8. Ages 50–55: Awakening.   Awakening—and then, with luck, enlightenment—springs from being able to see the world as it really is, and we cannot do this until we first pass through what psychologist Daniel Levinson called the process of *de-*illusionment. We spend most of our lives responding to illusions implanted during childhood. As children—and then as adults—we

- associate a police uniform with the notion of even-handed justice;
- see the priest or rabbi as a conduit to God;
- link the charismatic politician with great concern for human progress.

By fifty or so, however, we can see through the illusions created by uniforms, symbols, and razzmatazz, and are able to gauge the quality of the people filling these roles. Now, we know that all too frequently the policeman was (and still is) the bully boy from school; the priest an ineffectual dreamer; the all-wise politician just an aging actor reading cue cards.

De-illusionment is an emotional and spiritual experience that seldom occurs until we have come to a stage when we can truly apprehend our mortality, and have reached a conscious understanding of how to invest meaning into life's later years. This is an idea enshrined in many religions and cultures. Christians sometimes refer to it as a moment of epiphany akin to being "born again." Japanese call it *Satori.* Sensitivity training groups refer to getting "It." And fairy tales tell of a prince or princess wakening to a wonderful new life from a wicked spell (which, by the way, can be equated to the notion of a poisoned psychic contract).

Stage 9. Somewhere Beyond 50 or So: Perseveration or Renewal. Perseveration is the process of persisting in an activity after the meaning has gone from it. Thus, many successful executives persevere in the task of making a dollar long after the need for the dollar has gone. They dodge the deeper challenges of life by keeping the blinders on, and continuing to strain at the harness.

Should such people be out playing golf instead? Yes, of course—but maybe not all the time, for as Shakespeare observed:

> *If all the days were playing holidays,*
> *To sport would be as tedious as to work.*

The purpose of recreation is to take time out to re-create our selves, by developing the skill to play a good game, feeling at one with nature, and sharing our activities and our *selves* with friends.

Ultimately, however, we need to feel that what we are doing will also make some kind of difference to the world, albeit slight.

Thus, the real challenge of life is not to discover the meaning of life, but to address a far more practical question: "How can *I* give meaning to *my* life?"

When we can live without illusions, and know the value of a sunset, we realize that happiness—perhaps even sanity—depends upon finding our own answer to this question. Carl Jung said that all the many middle-aged men he treated suffered from the same problem: they wanted him to offer them some form of religion. The problem, however, is to renew life by investing it with meaning, not just with religion—and our meaning cannot come from someone else's prescription. As Lao Tse remarked, "The way that can be described is not the way."

We must learn to discount the stern parental voice of conscience, and listen to our own *selves* instead. We must hear and heed the small voice we used to hear in childhood. This may sound easy, but, all too often, it cannot be achieved until better than half our lives have passed. At that point, good news can come in the discovery that there are some tricks that only old dogs can learn.

Stage 10. Contributing for the Pleasure of It—The Latter Years.   The elder statesman enjoys a special place in our hearts. She is no longer a conniving politician, pushing sefish political interests. She has been through the mill. She has done it all and seen it all. She has made her mark, and been admired for so doing. She may even have fallen from grace at some time, and then risen like a phoenix from the ashes. Now, however, we see with our own eyes that she is both old and wise, a Mother Earth with much to offer. Her motivation is no longer power for its own sake but, instead, finally, the straightforward good of humankind— she just wants to contribute.

This is the role of the corporate guru. This role, which may or may not enjoy a title or formal authority, is the final and sometimes most personally fruitful stage of a business career.

How to play out such a role is still a matter of individual choice, of course. Former U.S. presidents have each addressed the challenge of the latter years according to their own style. Johnson retired a beaten man. Nixon redeemed himself—or came very close. Ford took to the golf course. Carter devoted himself to his Center for International Studies, and Reagan gave speeches to the Japanese at $2 million per performance.

GENERAL DIRECTION

General direction is largely a matter of social mobility. As we saw earlier, in our westernized culture, people are conditioned to want to rise in the world according to occupation, ranging through craftsman, merchant, professional, and artist.

To measure general direction, we simply rank a subject's origins against his or her present and likely social status. The achiever from the "wrong side of town" usually wants to join some kind of imagined aristocracy of achievers—or *meritocracy*. The emigrants who left Europe for America shared this kind of motivation. The person who began with a silver spoon in her mouth might be less likely to want to make a stir in the world. So, too, the comfortable middle classes are usually more concerned with falling back than marching forward.

In America, people who "get up in the world" are lauded and lavished with praise. New York State's governor, Mario Cuomo, frequently reminds his listeners of his humble emigrant parents, not so much out of modesty as out of pride. In England, however, social ambition—and success in realizing that ambition—has traditionally been regarded as somewhat déclassé, perhaps even a crime against the Almighty, for, as the Victorian poet asserted:

> *The rich man in his castle,*
> *The poor man at his gate,*
> *God made them high or lowly,*
> *And ordered their estate.*

At the end of it all, social mobility can be defined as a function of conditioning, together with an underlying drive to realize our potential and assume some kind of "rightful" place in society—not such unworthy things to strive for, surely.

**GENERAL
DIRECTION**
CAN BE
CLASSIFIED
UNDER
**TWO
HEADINGS**

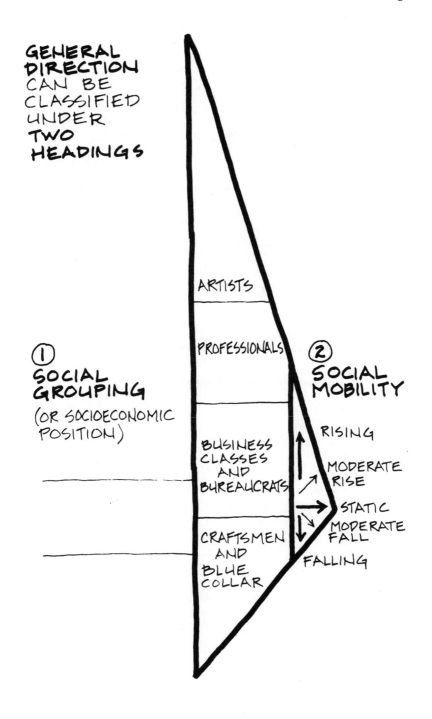

ARTISTS

PROFESSIONALS

① **SOCIAL
GROUPING**
(OR SOCIOECONOMIC
POSITION)

② **SOCIAL
MOBILITY**

BUSINESS
CLASSES
AND
BUREAUCRATS

RISING

MODERATE
RISE

STATIC

MODERATE
FALL

CRAFTSMEN
AND
BLUE
COLLAR

FALLING

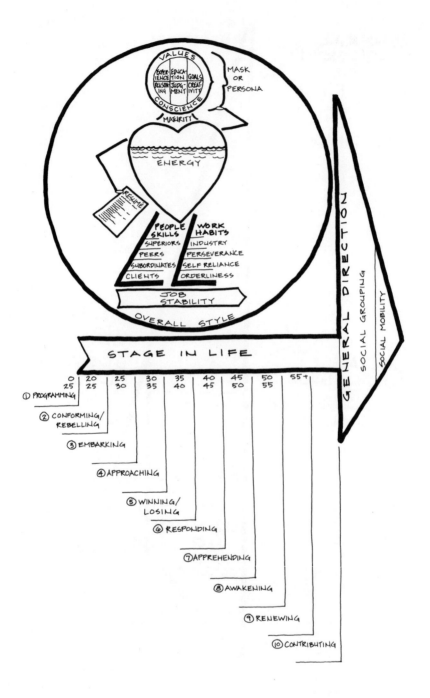

4

Sizing Up Great—
and Not So Great—
Executives

*How to Find Out
Everything You Need to Know
About an Executive,
and Make Deadly
Accurate Evaluations—
Time and Time Again*

Feather by feather, the goose is plucked.
JOHN RAY

Personnel decisions should never be made hastily. Consider:

- An American organization recently hired a convicted rapist in ignorance of his record—and was successfully sued for negligence by an existing employee who subsequently became another of the fellow's victims.
- George Bush thought he'd checked Dan Quayle out very thoroughly before promoting him as his running mate for the U.S. presidency. Yet somehow that check revealed neither Mr. Quayle's mediocre academic record nor his politically embarrassing failure to serve his country in Vietnam.
- A client of mine hired a woman who'd emerged that very day from a mental home—and who, alas, had to return just three months later.

Somebody has to hire such people, of course, and somebody should. But savvy executives are cognizant of the legal and ethical obligation—and the business necessity—of observing the doctrine of due diligence and taking pains to find out about the people they hire *before* the hiring.

Nonetheless, getting ahold of all the information can prove difficult and delicate, so mistaken judgments about executives inexorably continue to spring from the failure to uncover some key item of information—*usually because the missing piece of the puzzle was deliberately withheld or obfuscated.* So, remember this, dear reader:

- The *more* information you gather, the greater your chances of making a correct evaluation.
- The *less* information you gather, the more you risk making a mistake.

All of which leads us to what I call the Golden Rule of Executive Evaluation: *Don't appoint a pig-in-a-poke.*

Instead, make every reasonable endeavor somehow to get all the information you need to make a properly informed decision.

THE SYNDROME OF THE
ROMANTIC RUSH TO JUDGMENT

It is vital to withhold any final judgment about a subject—especially positive—until enough information has been gathered, because the syndrome of the romantic rush to judgment conspires to trip you if you don't:

> You start to "fall in love" with an idealized image of the subject, and, very soon, you can't bear to hear anything bad about the loved one. Then, those who report to you come to share your fuzzy feelings. They too can see no blemish in the blushing subject—or, if they can, they are loathe to thwart the romance, and bite their tongues. Finally, any person who continues to have misgivings, along with the temerity to *express* those feelings to the hirer, finds that either the unwelcome opinions fall upon deaf ears, or *the bearer of the bad news* becomes regarded with the kind of doubt and suspicion that should properly be directed at the loved one—hence the wisdom of Ambrose Bierce, who defined love as "A temporary insanity curable by marriage or by removal of the patient from the influences under which he incurred the disorder. It is sometimes fatal, but more frequently to the physician than to the patient."

There are many ways to collect information. You can have lengthy discussions or interviews with your subject, at work, in a social or recreational setting, perhaps even at his or her home. You can solicit information from superiors, peers, subordinates, customers and suppliers, past employers, from old schoolteachers and chums, from neighbors and members of the PTA, from a spouse or ex-spouse. You can have someone run a credit check. You can refer the subject to an assessment center. You can do any or all of these things, and a whole lot more as well.

However, there is no one best way to collect information. As long as you get it ethically, the precise methodology is not terribly important, just so long as you get it somehow.

THE TWO BASIC APPROACHES TO EVALUATION

Since most evaluators do not know what qualities they're seeking in a subject, they seldom know what kind of information to seek, or how to interpret whatever data is proffered.

The kind of information you'll seek—and how you'll go about collecting it—will be largely determined by whether you are sizing up an existing colleague or a potential new recruit. Let's consider this a little further.

There are two basic approaches to building an accurate understanding of an executive: working from the outside in, or from the inside out. Let's see what that means.

Method 1.   Working *from the outside in* means you observe the person's actual habits of behavior and attempt to identify meaningful patterns. We do this most of the time with existing colleagues, superiors, and subordinates. Then we flesh out the profile with knowledge of the value system that we gain through social interreactions.

Method 2.   Working *from the inside out* means that we discover the subject's life history and values, formulate a model of his/her psyche, and use this to predict his/her behavior patterns. We usually have to use this method to evaluate candidates for employment, and other strangers. Normally we supplement such an approach by calling some past employers and having them comment on actual behaviors.

HOW TO SIZE UP
THE EXISTING COLLEAGUE

*To succeed in the world, it is much more necessary
to possess the penetration to discern who is a fool,
than to discover who is a clever man.*
TALLEYRAND

A quick rule of thumb in these matters is that spotting
competence—and the potential for promotion—is difficult. It is smarter and more efficient to adopt the practice
of making *negative selections,* i.e., spotting and discarding
the least competent people, until finally you are left with
the person who is least likely to foul up!

This might not sound like a very daring way to run a
business, but it is likely to prove the most effective. Thus,
in sizing up an existing colleague, the savvy evaluator will
usually endeavor to reach a judgment by:

1. acquiring an understanding of the underlying
   causes of incompetence;
2. considering the executive's actual level of results;
3. identifing tell-tale signs of incompetence;
4. rating key managerial behaviors, and fleshing this
   out by obtaining background material on the subject if possible.

UNDERSTANDING THE
UNDERLYING CAUSES OF INCOMPETENCE

Management is often puzzled when considering incompetent executives, for such people are usually longtime
employees who know the industry, work hard, and look
good. They just fail to achieve results. Why is this? Well
may you ask. Well, here is the answer:

*Incompetence springs not from technical or intellectual shortcom-
ings, but from emotional factors. No matter how good he or she
might look, somehow, the incompetent executive just hasn't got
his/her head on straight.*

Spotting the underlying problem is rendered doubly difficult by what I call the Syndrome of the Heartless Lion. The incompetent executive, like the Cowardly Lion on his way to the Land of Oz, makes special efforts to seem to be a tough, macho executive—whereas the brave facade usually masks passivity, dependence, and anxiety.

This whole syndrome is well illustrated in the story of the woman who sought a job in the circus. She was assigned a lion's suit and given the task of prowling around inside a lion's cage, scaring the children and parents who had paid to see the lion. This proved to be an enjoyable job, until one day in the middle of her prowling and growling she glanced over her flank and realized that her cage door— which adjoined the cage of a fierce Bengal tiger—had swung open. The terrified "lion" immediately sprang to the bars of her cage and called to her audience for help, crying: "Save me, save me, I'm not a lion, I'm just a woman trying to earn a living!" Alas, however, attracted by the noise, the Bengal tiger immediately bounded into her cage, eyes blazing, teeth bared. Its claws sought her head, and its teeth her ear. Then it murmured: "Shut your mouth, you fool, or we'll both be out of a job!"

You should be advised that many companies are staffed on this basis, and that a lot of elegantly suited, apparently very macho "executives" are merely frightened wimps trying to scare up some respect in the threatening corporate jungle. If you could get behind the mask, you might discover eight basic problems.

An Incapacitating Underlying Fear of Failure. The fear of failure often renders an otherwise very ambitious person incompetent, because (a) the fear of failure is stress-provoking in and of itself; and (b) the act of imagining failure renders it much more difficult to work toward success.

An Incapacitating Fear of Success. Many people instill a fear of success into their children. They accomplish this by subtly warning that success may entail a loss of friends, imbuing a sense of unworthiness, suggesting that it is not right to "rise too far," and implanting the idea that "the higher one climbs, the more unpleasant will be the inevitable fall." The person who suffers a fear of success is therefore typically bedeviled either by an inability to seize opportunity, or, on becoming successful, by suffering self-doubt and guilt that provokes unconscious acts of self-sabotage.

A Fear of Ambiguity.   As noted, many conformists are crippled by an inability to perform in the absence of a structured environment. Paradoxically, such people are often very well educated. They are also hard workers, who shine in the lower echelons of management. They usually perform extremely well in training programs, where the situation is usually akin to an extension of the classroom environment.

An Alarming Tendency Toward Wishful Thinking.   In the face of difficulty, many overdependent executives cope by resorting to what they call "positive thinking." Their apparent optimism can be contagious, and may even be mistaken for "nerves of steel." In fact, such cheer typically reflects poor judgment and an underlying inability to face reality. By contrast, the savvy, well-adjusted executive tempers the need to put on a good face with realistic, practical steps toward achieving his or her goals.

A Chronic Perfectionism.   A perfectionist has been defined as a person who takes great pains, and gives them to others. How true this is. Perfectionists are driven by a neurotic need to deny their insecurities, and thus set unrealistically high standards and then drive themselves into a frenzy to meet them. They usually rationalize their neuroses as a "drive for excellence." They expect others to share their outlook, and if they do not, they become judgmental and angry. Their low opinion of the standards of others usually renders them very poor delegators and decision makers. They put off beginning a project, fearing they will never be able to get it exactly right, and they procrastinate in the face of an overwhelming search for the "right" decision. Finally, they run out of time. Then, since *nobody* could be expected to attain any kind of perfection, they feel free to jump in and push everyone to work like crazy—exactly like crazy!—and meet the seemingly impossible deadline. And so it goes. . . .

An Executive Senility.   Many executives suffer a loss of mental skills with the passage of time, becoming rigid, unable to deal with new concepts, frightened of change, resentful of younger executives, defensive, and, very simply, incompetent either to think or to act in a changing world.

A Lack of Desire to do the Job.   Sometimes a person may be too well balanced to be driven by any need to show strong achievement. Paul M was such a person. The son of a craftsman, he joined a large manufacturing organization, and showed such strong managerial skills that he soon found himself in the upper levels of management. The company wanted to appoint him to an even more senior role, but he refused, explaining that he was entirely fulfilled in his present job—which by the way entailed supervising a large group of craftsmen just like his father. He had more money than he needed, and he simply wanted to widen his leisure interests and enjoy his family.

Ambivalence Toward the Job or the Employer.   This is related to lack of desire, but more complex. Many intelligent, well-educated, but emotionally overdependent people are attracted by the rewards and apparent collegiality of the corporate world. They soon discover, however, that they are pitted against—and ill-suited to compete with—go-getting colleagues in a survival-of-the-fittest contest for profit and promotion. The overdependent ones usually only make it to lower middle management roles, but hang on for the security and the prestige. Soon enough, they become angered at their own dependence, envious of the former colleagues who got ahead, and resentful of the corporation for their predicament. Outwardly, such people—who often become long-serving employees—seem to be among the most loyal and dedicated. Inwardly, however, they often hate the company, detest their own jobs, and get even by steadfastly with-holding better than marginal competence.

CONSIDERING THE ACTUAL LEVEL OF RESULTS

Generally, competent executives show good results and incompetent executives show poor results. Sometimes an essentially incompetent executive can achieve very good results, but usually only at great personal cost either to her health or to her relationships. A truly competent person should not break down or die when the task is completed.

Overall, however, results are a good index of competence. And no matter how great they may look, or how many alibis they may offer, executives who consistently fail to achieve reasonable goals are likely to be incompetent.

IDENTIFYING TELL-TALE SIGNS OF INCOMPETENCE

The incompetent executive is often highly adept at finding ways to avoid taking responsibility without undue loss of face. Common facesavers include:

Proffering Plausible Pretexts. Otherwise incompetent executives often demonstrate an almost breathtaking ability to proffer creative rationalizations for their inability to produce results, which may be variously attributed—for openers—to fickle clients, falling market, fading product appeal, or fearsomely feisty foes.

Passing the Buck. This is a knee-jerk favorite of most of the run-of-the-mill incompetents you are likely to encounter working in medium-to-large organizations. Variations are many, of course, but generally the incompetent will

- Entice the boss to become involved and suggest a solution. This is sometimes called "the upward delegation of responsibility."
- Delegate the problem to a committee, then wait—and wait, and wait—for it to make a recommendation.
- Practice an extreme version of democratic participative management and delegate the problem to subordinates—"putting the inmates in charge of the asylum."

- Shunt the problem to another department—the "horizontal integration of responsibility."
- Send for a consultant to be scapegoated if things go wrong. This is sometimes called "getting in the guru and grasping for the gonads."
- Initiate a research study. ("We must get *all* the facts, no matter how long it takes.")
- Install a sophisticated computer system—to process all the data—then protest but go along, saying, "The computer made me do it."

Denying the Problem.   Protesting that the issue is unimportant, or was settled a long time ago.

Giving an Answer in Double-talk.   (If this is true, then we do this or that, except under this or that circumstance, when we do the opposite, but not all the time.)

Counseling Indefinite Delay of Action.   ("We must crawl before we walk, and walk before we run.")

Taking Flight into Detail.   Being too busy dealing with the problem to make a decision on how to resolve it.

Looking for an Answer in the Book—   "the bureaucrat's delight," since he or she has to do what the book says. And, of course, if the contingency is not covered in the book, no action can be taken!

Dissolving the Problem in Alcohol.   Finding the courage to make a decision in the bottom of a bottle. The world seems a far less threatening place when viewed through such a prism.

Falling Ill.   Coming down on the job with a stress-related ailment, such as a migraine headache or ulcer. Such psychogenic ailments inevitably meet five criteria:

- Cause the executive to be taken off the job for a while, either to go home or perhaps to enjoy a vacation.

- Shield the executive from insight into the true nature of her incompetence. She says, "I cannot perform my job because I have this ulcer." In fact, she has the ulcer *because* she cannot perform the job.
- Command sympathy from the executive's colleagues. Social conventions dictate that everyone treat him nicely—and, especially, not attempt to discuss his underlying incompetence.
- Punish him by exchanging a specific illness for a previously generalized anxiety.
- Shift the blame for the illness—and the underlying incompetence—to the employer. "I was unmercifully overworked."

Fleeing the Scene.   Being absent till the crisis has passed, getting called out of town, entering a series of urgent meetings, attending a series of seminars, taking a "sabbatical," or, ideally, taking a job with a competitor.

RATING KEY MANAGERIAL BEHAVIORS

A useful way to begin to size up an executive is to compare his (or her) actual behavior with behavioral patterns routinely demonstrated by successful managers. You can also have other key people—including the executive himself—rate the frequency of such behaviors.

The beauty of involving the executive himself in the exercise is that you can apprise him of his "blind spots" and set him to work at correcting them.

THE SAGA OF SIDNEY SHELL

Sidney Shell joined the smallest office of a young, growing real estate company as a salesperson. A direct fellow, with an outgoing personality, he was well liked by clients and colleagues. His sales performance wasn't great, but he had a lot of animation. When one day the branch manager quit, Sidney got the nod and took over.

Sidney enjoyed his authority, looked like a real leader, and was happy to devote long hours to the administration of his office. Soon, he was prodding top management with memos outlining ideas for overall expansion. He was very critical of the performance of a major regional office, which he felt was not showing appropriate results. Sidney's own office achieved only modest profits, but as Sidney quickly explained, this was a function of the very small market in which he labored. One day, upon receiving yet another of Sidney's memos criticizing the company's major office, the group vice president called Sidney. "You're right," he said. "Their performance is ordinary. Would you like to take over that branch?" Sidney took the relocation to this new major city.

Sidney decided to implement some new ideas. He installed new systems and fired a few "hacks"—salespeople who had shown consistent results, but who didn't fit with the new image that Sidney had in mind for the branch. Sidney commissioned an outside consulting firm to advise upon the image enjoyed by the company in the market. He also updated the company's premises, making them more in keeping with the upmarket clientele he felt the company should be seeking. Overall results failed to improve, but everyone agreed that Sidney looked comfortable in the role and was giving good direction. Then the fellow who took over Sidney's old branch began, as Sidney put it, "to capitalize on all of my hard work," turning in excellent figures and developing the branch into a major profit center.

When the group vice president was killed in a motor accident, everyone agreed that Sidney was the logical choice to take over. He had matured, he looked more like a leader than ever, he could be forceful, he liked being in charge, and he was a good administrator. Sure, he'd failed to achieve much in the way of profits, but he was not personally to blame. There'd been a downturn, and when the upturn came, everyone accepted that Sidney's branch would turn in figures consistent with his leadership stature and posture. And, since Sidney's own income was tied to profits, he seemed to have a powerful incentive to show good figures.

Sidney got the job; but, alas, the upturn never came. Instead, things got worse. His branch began to lose sales.

Suddenly, Sidney became embroiled in an argument with the company controller over accounting procedures, which Sidney said failed to reflect the true profit picture. "Either he goes, or I go," said Sidney.

An outside consultant was retained to address the problem, and summed it up this way:

Results: *Sidney's actual results consistently suggest an underlying incompetence. A true leader would not consistently produce mediocre results.*

Behaviors: *Sidney scores on many leadership behaviors, but falls short on some of the more crucial, including*

- *Setting goals and pressing for results.* He consistently sets low goals.
- *Relationships with superiors.* Sidney excells in getting along with his superiors. Indeed, he possesses a major skill in diverting attention from his modest accomplishments.
- *Customer liaison.* Sidney makes a good initial presentation with a client, but fails to win long-term confidence.
- *Setting priorities.* He fails to focus on the need to get out of the office and bring in business.
- *Dealing with ambiguity.* Sidney appears to lack the ability to deal with abstracts, or to set up new strategies in a changing environment.

Facesavers: *Facesaving tactics include*

- *using his imposing physical presence to quell questions;*
- *producing memos to divert attention elsewhere;*
- *focusing upon appearances rather than reality; and*
- *blaming the overall business environment.*

Underlying causes and interpretation: *Sidney is a first-born child with a naturally dominant style. He looks and behaves like a natural leader. In fact, he is a very conformist person, who lacks the ability to process information in a changing world. Though he is motivated by power, he cares comparatively little for actual results. He enjoys a very modest lifestyle, with a concomitantly low financial comfort level. He neither needs nor wants to earn a lot of* *money. He can no longer face his inability to actually produce, and is unconsciously seeking a way out.*

This "outside in" behavioral approach does not attempt to explore the executive's emotional makeup, underlying goals, or stage in life. You can either flesh this out later, or, sometimes, leave well alone! If, however, you are considering appointing the executive to a new and more demanding role, you will probably want to seek even more information, by using the second method set forth below and working from the "inside out."

SIZING UP THE NEW RECRUIT (AND/OR FLESHING OUT YOUR UNDERSTANDING OF THE VALUE SYSTEM OF THE EXISTING EMPLOYEE)

> *Bring me men to match my mountains,*
> *Bring me men to match my plains,*
> *Men with empires in their purpose,*
> *And new eras in their brains.*
> SAM WALTER FOSS

As a practical matter when facing a hiring decision, in order to discover the information you need, it is wise to run a series of interviews with the candidate.

Never hire an executive on the basis of only one interview, as some mediocre people can look great in just one meeting, and some quite excellent people can be slower out of the blocks. Ideally, I suggest four interviews, in at least three differing settings. Many candidates won't make it past the first interview, of course, and most will fall out—or drop out—prior to the fourth.

The primary reason for running several interviews is to get behind the mere persona and discover the real person, whose identity often unfolds as you move from one interview to another, and especially from the formality of the office to the apparent informality of a social situation. The four interviews I suggest are:

1. A brief "informal" interview. A good evaluator can often pick up a tremendous amount of information in twenty minutes or so. Never enough to make a decision to hire, but often enough to lose interest.
2. A "formal" office interview, which may take an hour or two, or longer. During this process you may also want to have the candidate meet some of his or her likely peers.
3. A "social" interview, perhaps over lunch, a game of golf, or somesuch. (This, of course, is also a wonderful way to gain greater insight into an existing colleague.)
4. Finally, if you're still interested, and can manage it, an interview in the candidate's home in the presence of his or her significant other(s). (Again, this kind of opportunity often readily presents itself with the existing employee.)

You'll also possibly want to try to fill out the picture by making some reference checks. As mentioned, the value of such references can be questionable, but nonetheless, due dilligence demands that you make the calls. And we'll come to that later.

TWO KEY QUESTIONS AND THE FIVEFOLD GRADING

Before you start the discussion, be sure of what you're trying to discover. I've already dealt with that pretty thoroughly, but for the record, let's briefly hit it again. You want to answer two questions:

- *Can this person do the job?* Can-do qualities are mostly determined by education and experience. A mere glance at the résumé might provide most of the information you need to answer this question.

- *Will this person do the job?* This is a much tougher question. The answer will turn upon five aspects of the subject's value structure, traits, and emotional makeup.

  1. *Goals.* What does the subject want or need, or both? What is the underlying motivation? And, crucially, *can these goals and emotional needs really be satisfied by my job?* If the subject's basic goals and needs cannot be fulfilled on the job, then he or she will probably leave or, at the very least, be an unhappy worker.
  2. *Work Habits.* Industry, perseverance, self-reliance, and orderliness.
  3. *People Skills.* Ability to get on with superiors, peers, subordinates, and clients. Qualities of empathy, loyalty, social dominance, and tact. Well-developed abilities to listen, discuss, write, and advocate.
  4. *Common Sense.* The ability to make good guesses in tricky situations.
  5. *Emotional Adjustment.* The absence of immature thought processes and behavior patterns.

THE SEVEN-POINT PLAN

In order to grade the subject on the five qualities outlined above, you'll need some information. You'll have to ask some questions and get some specific answers. Here again, I suggest that you approach this task systematically and endeavor to discover the subject's entire life history, from the cradle until this moment. You may not succeed in meeting this goal, but the closer you get, the better you will become at evaluating people. You can run a very loose, apparently informal interview, flitting from subject to subject if you like, just so long as you ultimately cover seven elements of the subject's life. I call this the Seven-Point Plan. Just take a sheet of paper and write the seven subheads down, then make your notes under each category.

Don't bother unduly to analyze your subject in terms of the fivefold grading until later. Just try to ensure that you cover the following seven areas of his or her life:

1. Employment history
2. Education
3. Upbringing
4. Finances
5. Significant other(s)
6. Health
7. Goals—and vocational summary.

The reason for hitting all the bases is quite simple: *You never know what you'll discover until you get into the conversation.* A paradox comes into play, here: *Because the subject knows what she wants to hide from you, she is more likely to reveal it*—just so long as you somehow bring the overall area into the conversation. It is hard to keep a secret. We want—and often feel compelled—to reveal ourselves to sensitive, understanding people. The secret comes into the forefront of consciousness and begs to be revealed. The sensitive evaluator senses that the subject wants to unload something, and reflexively pauses. The change in pace causes the subject to feel that the evaluator might have read his or her mind. Next thing you know, the whole thing is pouring everywhere.

THE OFFICE INTERVIEW

> . . . *hath been so clear in his great*
> *office, that his virtues will plead*
> *like angels trumpet tongued*
> SHAKESPEARE, *MACBETH*

You conduct a first brief interview because, often, that's all that either party will need to make a sound decision to go no further. The aim here is to establish common goals and, perhaps, some good chemistry. You are also honoring the social convention that smart people don't reveal too much of themselves to strangers. The conversation is thus a get-ting-to-know-you thing, wherein it is tacitly agreed that you'll both touch the high spots, and then come back later to really dig into things in the course of an "in-depth" interview. So, feel free to leave some items and come back to them later, if and when you still feel like proceeding.

Now let's look at the specific questions to which a smart evaluator would like answers, before giving any go-ahead to hire.

1. EMPLOYMENT HISTORY

Young men passed above his head
and rose and rose; but he was
always at the bottom.
CHARLES DICKENS, *DOMBEY AND SON*

I'd like you to tell me about your past employment, beginning with your first job and ending with your present job. I'd like to know how you got each job, the dates you worked there, your salary history, how you got on with the people, your management style, what you liked and disliked, what you accomplished, and how you came to leave.

Dates. Get the month and year of employment! This may become *very* important. You cannot spot a gap in employ-ment if you do not get these dates. Be wary of the subject who says he cannot remember them. Try to jog that reluc-tant memory. *Well, now, let's think about it a little. Did you join your new employer in the spring or the fall? Before the holiday season or after it?*

Salary History. As a rule of thumb, people are paid what they're worth. Thus, a top earner is usually doing a lot right and a low earner is probably turning in a mediocre per-formance. There are exceptions, of course, and in my expe-rience this rule is more likely to err on the side of overpaying. Thus, serendipity is more likely to account for a high income than a low income. Both cream and certain kinds of scum come to settle at the top.

Relationships.   Explore the four key areas: peers, subordinates, superiors, and customers. The well-adjusted person doesn't usually have too much trouble getting along with anyone. She identifies with the organization, and is happy to be a member of the team. She says *we* did this and *we* did that.

Listen carefully for signs of hostility, for while resentment might be justifiable, a truly smart person seldom criticizes a past employer. Such hostility reflects on a subject's common sense and emotional adjustment, as well as his qualities of empathy and loyalty. Remember, too, that hostility is readily displaced. Today it is directed at a past employer; tomorrow it may be directed at you.

Take special care to discuss the relationships with superiors, for a superior might just be mostly responsible for the fine performance of an otherwise mediocre subordinate. Find out how closely the job was structured, and how frequently the superior monitored progress.

Listen carefully as an executive discusses her management style, and try to fit it under the Dominant, Detached, Dependent framework. Fret (inwardly) when executives describe themselves as leaders, for just as a gentleman may be defined as a person who never uses the word, so, too, real leaders tend to let their accomplishments speak for themselves. Fret, too, if the word "aggressive" peppers their conversation—"I'm an aggressive hands-on executive," "I'm a demanding executive who pursues results very aggressively"—for macho words are often euphemisms employed by frightened souls who seek to rationalize their capacity to become ill-tempered under pressure.

Progress.   In considering titles and duties, listen for evidence of increased responsibility and matching income adjustment in each job. Good people usually get promoted—and financially compensated—fairly quickly.

Likes and Dislikes.   Likes and dislikes can reveal many things—including work habits, people skills, adjustment problems, and ability to cope under pressure, along with emotional needs for autonomy, achievement, power, status, and so on.

Achievements. In considering where the emphasis is placed on work accomplishments, you can usually begin to get a fairly good insight into what motivates a person. The Power Seeker emphasizes titles and numbers of people supervised; the Affiliator may emphasize how he or she was able to help others; and the Achiever will usually focus on specific, quantifiable, bottom-line results.

Reason for Leaving. People leave employers for many reasons. What you want to discover is precisely who precipitated the departure. Bear in mind that good people are very hard to find, so a smart employer will usually go to a lot of trouble to keep a good executive happy. On the other hand, the mediocre executive is usually pushed, one way or another, to look elsewhere. If the reason for leaving sounds a little weak, then, in the absence of evidence to the contrary, it is usually wise to assume that the employer is a smart operator who probably chose—one way or another— not to make it attractive for this particular employee to remain on in his or her job. Sometimes even savvy employers mistakenly let some very good people leave, of course. But not too often.

2. EDUCATION

In the dark ages great men often appeared. In those days only a man whom nature had expressly marked for greatness could become great. Now that education is easy, men are drilled for greatness, just as dogs are trained to retrieve. In this way we've discovered a new sort of genius, those great at being drilled. These are the people who are mainly spoiling the market.
GEORGE C. LICHTENBERG

I'd be interested to hear more about your education. Your favorite and least favorite subjects. How you ranked academically, which subjects you liked best and least, your extracurricular activities, any special scholarships or prizes, any positions to which you were elected, what you regard as your greatest achievements during your education, and how your education was financed. Maybe we could begin with high school and then talk about college.

Education can be a useful field in which to furrow. Talking about education also naturally opens up a general discussion of family life and influences. Look for

Overall Style Patterns. The Dominant, Detached, and Dependent patterns can show up very early. The associated drives for power and status, achievement and autonomy, affection and achievement can sometimes be particularly easy to spot.

Evidence of Commitment and Perseverance. Follow the reasoning behind any decision not to complete an examination or degree.

Interest in Hard-nosed Practical Subjects. These include business, psychology, science, and so on. The broader liberal subjects—literature, philosophy, history—appeal to complex, sensitive students who like to speculate upon abstract issues. People who excell in business are often more likely to be attracted to more down-to-earth—as they see it—subjects.

Extracurricular Activities. Wide interests help to round a person out. Activities such as chess, debating, and photography may reflect an inquiring mind, creativity, or strong self-improvement needs.

Election to Leadership Roles. Many opportunities for election to leadership roles arise in college. Election to such roles may signal early natural leadership ability, or strong affiliation needs.

Grades. This is often a very good index of motivation and achievement needs. Don't jump to the conclusion, however, that high grades are synonymous with overall good judgment. The two may have nothing in common.

Financial Contribution. The student who must find money to help pay the bills often learns to become self-reliant and mature more quickly than the student who does not. The contribution may come in the form of winning scholarships and the like.

Vacation Activities. These can tell you a lot about motivation. Was the subject out on the beach, or was she out working hard to finance herself? The truly savvy, focused individual may have used the opportunity to take up a summer internship in the area of her major career interest.

Entrepreneurial Bent. Of particular interest is the student who established some kind of business while at college. This is one of the better indices of real executive potential.

3. UPBRINGING

The human being cannot live too long in the bosom of his family without serious dangers to his psychic health.
CARL JUNG

I see you attended school in XYZville. Do you still have roots there? Did any of your brothers and sisters go to the same school or college? Do you see them much these days?

If you followed the material in Chapter 3 of this book, you'll realize that most people's lives are programmed for them during childhood. So, to determine that programming, along with the psychic contract and the potential culminating achievement, you'll want to discover:

- *The socioeconomic positioning of the family,* as evidenced by the occupations and interests of the parents.
- *The values they promoted.* Did they instill the work ethic? The achievement motive?
- *The emotional climate in the home.* A happy home usually produces happy people; an unhappy home produces unhappy people. Separations and divorces often signal an unhappy emotional climate.
- *Relationships with parents.* Well-adjusted people usually enjoy good relationships with both parents. Poor relationships with parents usually suggest an unhappy emotional climate.
- *The relationship of the family to the community.* Apparently underprivileged families have an uncanny knack of producing outstanding achievers. The children of well-to-do parents will be motivated by an entirely different set of social expectations.
- *The subject's place in the family.* Eldest, middle, youngest? How much effect has this had on the development of an overall personality style? What are the occupations of the siblings? Does the subject seem to be maintaining his or her place in the family?

Frankly, a savvy and subtle evaluator could get answers to all of the above questions, and a lot more too, in that first twenty-minute interview—without pushing or even seeming to do so. Armed with this information, plus salary and job history, that evaluator would be well on the way to establishing an understanding of the subject's psychic contract and likely destiny.

4. FINANCES

Get to know two things about a man—
how he earns his money and how he spends it—
and you have the clue to his character,
for you have a searchlight that shows up
the innermost recesses of his soul.
You know all you need to know about his standards,
his motives, his driving desires, and his real religion.
ROBERT J. McCRACKEN

I see you live in XYZville. How do you find the commute? How did you come to discover that lovely area? I believe some good property values are to be had there.

The commute question is really great, because it can seem like mere friendly banter, but the time it takes to get to work is clearly a very relevant item and the response usually opens the conversation to the even more relevant matter of

Financial Comfort Level. You want to discover how much money the subject needs to support his or her life-style. Will the income package that you are offering cover the subject's outgoings? Does the lifestyle indicate prudence or indulgence? Are sights set so low as to provide little or no incentive to chase sales and profits? Are the earnings expectations realistic?

Does the subject own or rent? One home, or more? One car, or more? Other toys and goodies? Are there kids to support and put through college? What kinds of colleges are they shooting for? Ideally, you want some figures, cost of the home(s) and the amount of the mortgage(s), the approximate monthly outgoings, and the approximate net worth. You can usually induce the subject to proffer you these figures, or enough information for you to make an intelligent guess. In the event of a demurral don't worry, just make a mental note of the reticence, and proceed to the other areas. Later on, if you still have an interest in the subject, simply run a credit check prior to any offer to hire.

You'll also want to address the question of whether the subject has already outstripped the socioeconomic positioning of his or her own parents, and, if so, whether this might suggest any kind of tapering off, or burning out.

THE CASE OF THE
SIDETRACKED SALESMAN

Chancey Climbing (thirty-eight) a very charming big ticket salesperson was being considered for promotion to marketing director. He failed to produced much in the way of sales during his year in the field, but this was attributed to a necessarily long lead time. A routine interview revealed that in the past two years Chancey had acquired no less than eight homes on a no-money-down basis. He also leased a yacht, and a sportscar. The cost of maintaining this high-flying lifestyle exceeded the maximum amount he would earn if he attained all of his sales targets! The conclusion, alas, was that Chancey's status needs and financial comfort level were so high as to compel him to devote virtually all of his energy to his own interests—running a real estate firm, in effect—and virtually no time at all to pursuing sales. In consequence, he didn't get the promotion, and was also taken off salary and rewarded on a straight commission basis. One month later he left the company.

---

5. SIGNIFICANT OTHER(S)

Do not choose your spouse at a dance, but in a field among the harvesters.
CZECH PROVERB

I guess with all those trees and open spaces it could be a very nice place to raise a family. Are there any good restaurants out there, or do you mostly entertain at home? Would there be any problems relocating?

It used to be that an executive was a male who was happily married to a female, who bore and raised wonderful kids. Divorce was a no-no, and homosexuality entirely sinful. Things have changed. Society, including the corporate world, is much more tolerant of diverse lifestyles. All sorts of people have come out of various closets and the closet of the supposedly happily married was the first to empty. Nowadays, a lot of executives have skipped marriage completely, either to live with one, or a series of partners quite openly. Others are divorced and remarried. Some are divorced and single. Some are gay, and may be married to gay partners. These days, with an acceptance of many lifestyles, we tend to worry for the mental health of people who remain rigidly intolerant of such changes.

However, if you want to come up with an accurate evaluation of an executive, consideration of his or her private living arrangements can become quite crucial, for the choice of significant other may profoundly affect an executive's

1. Outlook and goals
2. Financial comfort level
3. Geographic and social mobility
4. Ability to get along with others
5. Commitment to corporate life.

What you need to know, is whether the relationship will help or hinder the executive's ability to perform the job? As you consider this question there are two things to bear in mind: The significant other will almost certainly have yet another family destiny to fulfill. This can be determined pretty quickly by discovering:

1. The socioeconomic positioning of the significant other's parents.
2. The educational level of the significant other.
3. The significant other's place in the family. (Armed with this information you may be able to make a close enough stab at the style and underlying socioeconomic goals of the significant other.)

4. Shared interests and activities. Signs of a happy relationship, community consciousness, and, perhaps, upward mobility. Willingness to entertain clients may also be of interest.
5. Offspring produced, and goals envisioned for them. These will affect the financial comfort level.
6. Whether the significant other is the prevailing partner. If the significant other is the submissive partner, then the executive's agenda will probably take precedence. If the significant other is the prevailing partner, then the significant other's agenda will take precedence, and you'll want to make sure that these goals are congruent with your own.

Finally, a really good question to drop in, is, *Does your significant other have any little pet peeves or complaints about you?* This apparently innocuous question often yields a very insightful answer, which the executive—failing to apprehend the accuracy of his loved one's complaint—is often quite delighted to relate.

Two such responses spring to mind. One fellow who looked very good, confided that his wife complained that he was "submissive and indecisive." How right she was! Another interviewee cited a different pet peeve: "He hates the fact that whenever we get into an argument I'm always right."

"Are you always in the right?" I asked.

"Oh, yes, I'm always right! And he doesn't like it one little bit!"

In fact, it is seldom difficult to evoke a discussion about family and loved ones. Indeed, such a conversation normally opens up with a question about the commute. Once you have him speaking on this, it's usually fairly easy to collect much of the other information that you need. Well handled, such a chat can seem to be very casual and unimportant, almost like a digression or respite from weightier topics.

6. HEALTH

*A man too busy to take care of his
health, is like a mechanic
too busy to take care of his tools.*
SPANISH PROVERB

What kinds of things do you do to stay in shape?

Physical health is related to emotional adjustment. Unsound health thus often denotes emotional problems, and difficulty in dealing with stress. When the pressure of a job becomes too much, health problems often manifest themselves. Such problems include, headaches and migraines, asthma attacks, and stomach problems, including ulcers and colitis. People treat these problems in many ways, some with prescribed drugs, some with over-the-counter drugs, including, of course, alcohol and nicotine.

A good executive is likely to be more emotionally well-adjusted than most people, and therefore less prone to suffer health problems. Ultimately, smart executives typically take good care of themselves.

Thus in evaluating an executive, it is important to consider health, and, as a rule of thumb, to work on two assumptions:

- *Recurring health problems can indicate emotional difficulties, and problems in dealing with pressure.* Find out what kind of situations provoke the problem. Try to discover what kind of treatment is usually applied to help ease the problem.
- *The problem will probably recur if similar circumstances arise in the future.* Structure any job so as to prevent exposing the executive to that kind of situation in the future.

Two common medications are nicotine and alcohol, of course, so it is wise to discover whether an interviewee smokes or drinks, and, if so, how often, and when.

To find out about health problems, I suggest that you:

- Open up with a polite inquiry as to health, and let it run into a general discussion, during which you might "casually" wonder about accidents, hospitalizations, migraines, heart problems, ulcers, and the like.

  It would be foolish—not to mention illegal—to discriminate against a person merely because he or she is handicapped—crippled, blind, epileptic, suffering from AIDS, and so on. The test is whether or not a health problem manifests itself as a result of the kind of pressure that is an inherent part of the job.
- Require a full medical examination prior to employment, and a regular annual check up.

The other question to drop in at this point, is a polite inquiry as to the health of immediate family members. Often, a sick or troubled executive also brings along a sick or troubled family. This may be entirely unimportant. On the other hand, it may later come to constitute a very significant distraction. Best to find out early.

---

7. GOALS
–AND VOCATIONAL SUMMARY

> *Climb high*
> *Climb far*
> *Your goal the sky*
> *Your aim the star.*
> Inscription on Hopkins Memorial Steps,
> WILLIAMS COLLEGE

I'd be interested to hear about your greatest personal achievement, where you feel you might have failed, your immediate and longer range goals, including what you realistically hope to be earning five—and maybe even ten—years from now.

Greatest Achievement. Is the achievement job-related. What specific needs does it reflect. If an off-the-job achievement is cited, you'll need to check to see if the kind of effort that went into it can be channeled on the job.

Achievers will usually focus on some job-related achievement. Power seekers will focus on titles and the number of people managed. Affiliators will stress the relationships they have enjoyed, often focusing on marriage and raising children.

Failures. Again, it is useful to consider the answer in the light of the dominant, detached, dependent framework. The dominant individual often regrets a failure to win power or status, the detached individual regrets a loss of autonomy or achievement, and the affiliator pines for opportunities to develop relationships.

Many people find it hard to acknowledge failure, so the answer can also be used to calibrate a subject's insight and candor. Does the answer reflect an inability to accept reality? Is the subject an "alibi artist" who considers himself or herself a victim, and attempts to blame others when things go wrong?

Short and Long Range Goals. What psychological needs are reflected: power? status? achievement? security? autonomy? Do these goals sound realistic? Unrealistic goals are a prime index of the immature person who suffers from a tendency to wishful thinking. Are these goals congruent with the job and opportunities now under consideration? If not, can a workable compromise be reached?

Income Expectations. The subject is stating his or her projected comfort level. Does the response sound realistic? Will the envisioned career provide the opportunity to earn this kind of money? Might too low an expectation suggest lack of motivation?

THE SOCIAL INTERVIEW

An interview away from the office offers fresh opportunities to gain insights and information. Though apparently more relaxed than the office interview, the social interview can actually be more demanding, and rehearsed answers that might pass unnoticed in an office interview, may now sound banal and phony. Some hucksters are at their very best in such situations too, of course, so beware, and take care to gather hard data, as well as mere impressions.

The most common of such interviews is the luncheon interview. It is also relatively common to invite a subject to a game of golf, perhaps in a foursome with other interested parties. Special advantages of the social interview include:

The Ambiguity of the Situation.   Qualities of social intelligence and judgment come into play. Subjects are expected to reveal the more relaxed side of their personality, with a little good-natured banter and so forth. They must respond quickly and sensitively to the changing tones and moods. If a game of golf is being played, then the game itself naturally provides an opportunity to see the subjects perform under pressure. How they cope with a clumsy or embarrassing stroke, the extent to which they curse, fume, pout, or even cheat may be of particular interest. Such behaviors may inconclusively indicate either a low frustration tolerance, or a high need to achieve. Nonetheless the behaviors constitute new information for the evaluator.

The Infusion of Alcohol.   The evaluator now has an opportunity to question the subject as he becomes influenced by a consciousness altering drug. Thoughts, words and behavior will all be influenced. The everyday facade will surely slip. An attentive evaluator will glean new insights, and perhaps new information, too.

What if the subject is abstemious? Must he still swallow the proffered fluid? In the past, perhaps yes. Today, people are more enlightened. And, in this new age, a casual, "any particular reason?" could be made to sound like a solicitous query. Is the subject just a very sane, detached individual whose life is so together that alcohol is irrelevant. Or, might the manner of his refusal of the refreshment indicate obsessiveness or rigidity. Perhaps the subject is a recovering alcoholic, someone who has faced up to his problem and is *actually dealing with it.* Such a person might prove to be a very good bet indeed. The executive who orders both a glass of white wine *and* a glass of soda—and then simply "forgets" to drink the wine—might be marked up for social adroitness. The subject who embraces the opportunity to devour a couple of very expensive bottles of fine wine is probably best suited to a sales role, working on straight commission.

The Opportunity to Reveal Your Organization as Having Human Qualities. Smart executives know that organizations have personas too—and value any opportunity to explore the real personalities behind such facades. If you both come to like what you discover behind the exterior, then the path to a good working relationship may be significantly eased.

If you plan to conduct a social interview, you'll possibly want to keep the following caveats in mind:

Don't Set Out to Impress the Subject. Say who you are and be who you are. Treat the subject as you would like to be treated in such circumstances. You'll put your best foot forward, of course, and you'll also be entitled to press the advantages inherent in the situation—which any smart executive will appreciate. But play it straight.

Choose an Appropriate Venue. Check that the meal will be congruent with the subject's dietary preferences. Steak houses, and other one-fare establishments that used to be very popular among business people are not always suitable.

Don't entertain subjects at a club where they might not reasonably aspire to membership. Your purpose is to gather information, not to intimidate or embarrass. There is no particular problem in patronizing one of those restaurants that *pretends* to be a club, like New York's well known 21 Club. Even here, however, the ambience may prove distracting, for, often, the primary purpose of such a clientele is to draw attention to themselves.

Book a Suitable Table. The newspaper magnate, the late Lord Thompson of Fleet, reputedly favored taking subjects to one of London's famous pie carts for a stand up lunch.

The simplicity of the venue may have been an inspired choice, reflecting Lord Thompson's well known lack of pretension. The seating arrangements were probably not conducive to an intimate conversation, however, and I personally suggest booking a quiet corner table, suitable for an intimate conversation, in advance of any luncheon.

Be Punctual. Arrive on time and finish on time. Respect the subject's need to get back to the office. If the subject is coming from out of town then by all means show the courtesy of a good hearing. Show that your own organization appreciates both the importance of time, and the value of good human relations.

Press for Answers to Previously Unanswered Questions. The purposes of this interview are to collect even more information about the subject's life and career, to plumb his or her value structure, and, finally, all going well, to move toward cementing a working relationship.

The interview is best opened with generalities. It can be very smart to discuss tidbits served by the media concerning politicians of the day, for opinions concerning such figures reflect underlying values, along with attitudes toward authority. This is also an entirely suitable occasion to further probe upbringing, present circumstances, off-the-job interests, and overall goals. If unanswered questions concerning career-history continue to worry you, then bring these matters up in the latter stages of the interview when the subject is relaxed and expansive.

THE HOME INTERVIEW

Nobody shoulders a rifle
in defense of a boarding house.
BRET HARTE

The home interview has been a hot topic for years. In England, where a man's home has always been presumed to be an inviolable castle and retreat, the English still tend to gag on the notion of some evaluator—presumably a vulgar American—traipsing in to size up the family.

The pragmatic Americans, however, quickly realized that an executive's home situation vitally affects on-the-job performance, and included the home in the package of elements routinely to be considered when appointing a senior executive.

More recently, however, the home interview has been more talked about—and tut tutted over—than actually practiced. Just the same, if you are *really* serious about sizing up an executive, then a lot of information is to be gleaned from a relatively quick trek into his or her lair, for such an incursion provides all sorts of insights and information not readily available from other sources.

Actually getting into the home is usually a fairly straightforward matter. You simply explain to the subject that, since the job involves important long term career and lifestyle implications, both for the subject and the significant other, these important issues should be addressed. Then, when the subject agrees, and raises the question of how best to do this, you suggest dropping by the home to meet the significant other—perhaps prior to taking both partners to a restaurant. Factors to be considered during such a visit include:

The Neighborhood. A smart executive realizes the many advantages conferred by an upmarket neighborhood; high resale value, better schools, upwardly mobile people, and so on. A formerly decayed suburb now in the process of gentrification may also reflect good judgment on the part of its owner.

The Dwelling. It is usually a very simple matter to discern an executive's overall personality style and goals from a quick study of the home. The Dominant individual's concern with power and status usually reflects itself in the choice of furnishings and decorations. The Detached individual is more concerned with function. The Dependent individual displays photos of loved ones. Taste, judgment, and creativity, along with work habits and social sensitivity will also be reflected in the various aspects of the home.

The People Who Inhabit the Dwelling. Insight is offered into the number of dependents, the existence of whom might not have been previously mentioned. The subject's ability to keep these people in line, may also be of special interest. The presence of a pet or pets might also be of interest: A very lonely executive I once knew comforted himself with the presence of two Great Dane dogs, a Siamese cat, a large parrot, a snake, and a suitable supply of white mice.

The Prevailing Person. One individual usually dominates a relationship, and it is often a fairly simple matter to spot this Prevailing Person (PP) during the course of a home interview. Normally the PP controls the finances, decides the major purchases, chooses guests, vacation activities, and so on. If the subject is not the PP then you will want assurance that the challenges offered by your job are congruent with the goals of the PP, and that the PP is supportive of the subject. To accomplish this, it can be very useful to ask the PP to talk about his or her values, along with opinions concerning the "ideal" job for the submissive party.

Appraising the home situation necessarily calls for judgment on the part of the evaluator, but, in the final analysis, often only one question needs to be addressed:

Will the home situation help or hinder the subject's on-the-job performance?

5

Interpreting the Information Gathered

and
Resolving
the Jigsaw Puzzle
of the
Executive Profile

∞

The Master said, Look closely into his aims, observe the
means by which he pursues them discover what brings
him content—and can the man's real worth remain
hidden from you, can it remain hidden from you?

THE ANALECTS OF CONFUCIUS

A long time ago now, when asked to evaluate a sales executive in line for promotion to chief of a major cruise line, I had the candidate write out a brief autobiography. I was overseas when it came in, so it went directly to my colleague, Dr. (Doc) Robert N. McMurry. Soon enough he was on the phone: "What you've got here," he said, with considerable excitement, "is a mean, ruthless, son-of-a-bitch who would cut his own grandmother's throat to get ahead in the world."

"I have?"

"Yes, you've got a driven, status conscious, sweet-talking salesman, who will stop at nothing!"

"At nothing?"

"At nothing."

"You've got one of these strictly-from-New-York-boys, who knows all the angles, and would push anyone aside to get what he wants."

"Listen, Doc. Maybe you're right, but where are you getting all this from?"

"Did you ever read *What Makes Sammy Run?*"

"No, Doc, can't recall I ever did."

"Well, you should get it out and look at it, because what you've got here is another Sammy Glick."

There it was! Doc had absorbed the material, divined the style of dominant dependent, and further refined it into the subcategory of a Sammy Glick, Bud Schulberg's ruthless hireling newspaper boy who ultimately rises by dint of charm, cunning, chutzpah, and cheating to head a major Hollywood film studio.*

Sizing up an executive is like trying to solve a jigsaw

*If you'd like to know more about this subtype—along with many others—refer to Gonnabee, in *Wareham's Basic Business Types* (New York: Atheneum, 1987).

puzzle when you don't know what the final picture will look like—and don't have all the pieces to the puzzle.

Most people try to solve the puzzle too quickly. They fail to collect all available pieces, and clumsily try to force the few pieces they do have together, "willy nilly." No wonder they usually get it all wrong!

The smart operator, on the other hand, grabs as many pieces of the puzzle as possible at the outset (though still never *all* of them). He or she then studies the pieces, makes a guess at what the overall picture might be, and lays out the pieces to see if they fit this profile. If the pieces don't fit, the process is undertaken again. Finally, when the right profile has been identified, the evaluator uses his or her imagination to fill in the blanks.

The smart evaluator does much the same, collecting as much information as possible on the subject—examining, studying, and contemplating it—then blinking a couple of times, and—voilà!—an overall image of the subject appears upon the screen of the evaluator's mind. Finally, it is back to the the original data, to reinterpret it in terms of the overall image, fleshing out the portrait of the subject's personality and competence.

The smart evaluator thus brings the unconscious, creative process into play. The unconscious receives the data, runs it through the vast hopper of unconscious memory, comparing it with all the people the evaluator has ever known, finding the profile of the person who seems the closest fit, and then developing a new profile based upon that person. The evaluator's judgment—no less than yours or mine—is thus closely related to the entire *vocabulary* of people he or she has ever seen and contemplated. *And the purpose of this book, is to help you improve your capacity to reach an accurate final judgment by:*

- Permitting you to categorize your *existing* vocabulary of people within the Dominant/Detached/Dependent model.
- Using that same model as a basis for evaluating and classifying *additions* to your vocabulary of types.

How To Know When You've Really Solved the Puzzle

If the processes of collecting and considering the material, coming up with an overall profile, and reinterpreting the data to flesh out the profile all have been well executed, then the picture so disclosed will make such good sense that people to whom you relate your finding will usually agree wholeheartedly—often going so far as to tell you they knew it already!

If you get the overall profile wrong, however, then you'll probably get everything else wrong, too. Neither you nor your listener will be confident of your opinion, for your own unconscious will be telling you that your picture is somehow awry or out of focus. *This usually happens when your unconscious hasn't received enough material to come up with an accurate overall profile.* So, you must go back and get more information—more pieces to the puzzle.

SOLVING THE JIGSAW
PUZZLE, STEP BY STEP

Let's just summarize the process one more time, in simple steps:

- Collect as much information on your subject as you can.
- Take an overview of all the material.
- Try to identify the major motivation.
- Consider the cluster of needs.
- Try to establish the *overall style.*
- Go back to the original information and set about interpreting it again, this time in terms of the overall profile.
- If the picture you come up with seems wrong, then *go back and get more information*—and go through the whole process again.
- Don't stop until you feel that you have fleshed out a realistic *portrait of the subject.*

CLUES TO HELP YOU
SPOT THE PICTURE IN THE JIGSAW PUZZLE

Divining a portrait of the subject involves an unconscious process, but getting that process started, merely takes a conscious, systematic effort to:

- Identify the key need—and the likely cluster of needs.
- Analyze the subject's personality in terms of the Dominant/Detached/Dependent (M/T/P) framework.
- Determine the likely family destiny, including:

> Psychic contract
> Stage in life

To accomplish this, I suggest you contemplate the following chronological checklist of key clues from the subject's life.

1. *Parental socioeconomic positioning.*
2. *Place in the family.* Socioeconomic positioning of any siblings. How has this affected the subject's development and expectations?
3. *The psychic contract.* The core values. The prime parental directive. The tacit criteria of a successful life. The lifestyle expectation.
4. *Emotional climate in the home.* Relationships with parents. The underlying emotional condition. Might this have implanted a Golden Spur, or a Phaeton force?
5. *Education.* School and college behavioral patterns. Interests, achievements, social integration.
6. *Stated goals.* What might be the culminating achievement? The underlying need? The lifestyle expectation? The financial comfort level?
7. *Persona and presentation.* What impression does the subject most want to make?
8. *Choice of career, and history.* Consider industry, function, and the kinds of needs that entry to this career might satisfy.
9. *Stated management style.* Management style and overall personality style are usually very similar.

10. *Possessions.* House, car, and other key possessions will usually reflect the subject's personality.

11. *Significant other.* To what extent does the choice of significant other reflect the subject's underlying emotional needs?

12. *Golden spur.* Is there an intense, positive underlying drive that might have fostered a special "burning desire" to show great achievement.

13. *Does the subject sound like a winner or a loser?* Winners attain their goals, and fulfill the psychic contract. Losers fall short of the goals, fail to complete the contract, and usually blame others. At-Leasters almost attain their goals and offer half apologies.

THE CASE OF THE UNCOMFORTABLE EMIGRÉ

Consider an actual example here. Let's assume you've been asked to evaluate a subject who has applied for a senior marketing role in an important U.S. organization. He is currently holding a similar position with a competitor in South Africa where he grew up. He heard of the vacancy and asked to be considered.

Lesley Hartford (thirty-nine) was born in South Africa, the only son in a family of four children. He says his father, a senior army officer who later retired to purchase and manage a caravan park, was "a good man, but somewhat overbearing." He says his mother, a former schoolteacher, was "a delight, adorable." Lesley's sisters became, respectively, a nurse, a schoolteacher, and a secretary.

Lesley attended a local private school, and went on to study accounting at the local polytechnic. Upon graduation, his parents financed his successful full-time pursuit of a two-year master's degree in business.

At age twenty-five, Lesley left home and began work as a cost analyst and management accountant. Two years later he was appointed internal auditor, and held that position for three years.

At age thirty Lesley says he "gravitated to sales." He sought and was appointed to a sales vacancy in the company and proved an outstanding success, selling more equipment than any peer and doubling his income. Three years later he switched to a competitor firm, for a much higher base income and better commissions. Two years after that he was appointed sales manager. The company had a "hot" product. Sales were high for three years, at which point the competitors released an equivalent product and sales evened out. The marketing vice president took a job with a competitor, and Lesley was appointed to fill the vacancy. The role involved supervising 100 employees in marketing, sales, customer service, and overseas managers. Sales were steady but the company continued to lose much market share.

Lesley is critical of the short-term thinking of his superiors. He feels that senior management is stifling the marketing effort by not giving him the kind of budget he needs to establish a winning position in the market. He feels that the company must come up with a new breakthrough product urgently.

Lesley has been married for thirteen years. He says that his wife, a nurse, four years his senior, "is from a very good family, a social asset, and a good mother to our three young children."

Lesley and his wife own a large home that they have extensively renovated; it is mortgaged to 70 percent of its estimated value. They own two cars, a second-hand Porsche and a Volkswagen. They also own a small yacht, and have a 30 percent stake in a ski chalet. Their net worth is equal to the amount of their equity in their home.

Lesley's spare-time interests include skiing and membership in the local Junior Chamber of Commerce, where he pursues a keen interest in debating.

Lesley recently advised several "headhunters" that he would like to switch employers and take an overseas assignment.

Lesley says that he is very health-conscious and likes to work out regularly. He is a non-smoker, but "takes a couple of glasses of wine with dinner." He suffers mild facial eczema, which he says "comes and goes," along with "mild intermittent indigestion" and the "very occasional migraine."

During the course of your interview, he also notes:

- *My parents expected me to become an accountant, plan a safe future, and work toward financial independence. My father was a real man, and big on manly things, and planning. But he was very conservative. My own goal is to become self-employed, because that's where the real money is, and I feel I could be an outstanding success. I just need some good breaks.*
- *I am a democratic but very aggressive manager. I am a good leader. People like me. They also look up to me and respect me. They know I'm a winner.*
- *I've had about enough of my present employer. I'm stagnating. They don't truly appreciate the market. They're holding me back. They're living in a dream world, and expecting impossible results. How can you outsell anyone unless you have a better product?*
- *I've been thinking of going overseas for a year or so now. I'd like to make an entire new start. Maybe I'll find a whole new outlook in a new country. I might even look at something entirely different, something entrepreneurial. I am determined to succeed. I know I'm a winner.*
- *I work hard and play hard. I want to have the good things in life before it's all too late. I hate paperwork, and delegate it. I work forty to fifty hours a week. I'm at my desk at eight in the morning; nine if I've had a heavy night entertaining clients, or whatever.*
- *My strengths lie in my people skills. Almost everybody likes me. I have a gift with people. I can be stubborn, of course. You have to be stubborn to get results. I can be as aggressive as anyone. Nobody can push me around.*

Now let's examine all this material in terms of the items that will help us to determine Lesley's overall style.

1.	*Parental socioeconomic positioning.*	Father a senior army officer, later acquired and ran a caravan park. Mother a schoolteacher. *Stern father, nurturing mother.*
2.	*Place in the family. Sibling socioeconomic positioning.*	Three siblings, all female, all older. At least two *nurturing sisters.*
3.	*The psychic contract. The core values. The tacit criteria of a successful life. The lifestyle expectation. The prime parental directive.*	Middle-class values. Urged to seek professional career. *Financial independence also seems to have been valued.*
4.	*Emotional climate in the home.*	Speaks of his father with great respect, and some trepidation. Remembers his mother as being very loving, "a delight, adorable." *A need to win the father's respect and approval?*
5.	*Education.*	Attended a local private school and later studied accounting at the local polytechnic. Successfully pursued a two-year master's degree in business on a full-time basis—financed by his parents.
6.	*Stated goals.*	To "become self-employed . . . I feel I could be an outstanding success."
7.	*Persona and presentation.*	"I am determined to succeed. I know I am a winner." Is disingenuous, pleasing, and, for a thirty-nine-year-old, very boyish.

8.	*Choice of career, and history.*	Large company. Secure role in accounting. Gravitated to sales. *Charm and natural manipulative abilities?* Gets promoted to management, runs into dead end. "Stagnating." Seeking to quit. *Couldn't hack it in management. Probably being squeezed out.*
9.	*Stated management style.*	"Democratic but very aggressive . . . I can be as aggressive as anyone." *Wants to please people but becomes autocratic?*
10.	*Possessions.*	An extensively renovated home, mortgaged to 70 percent of its value. Owns two cars, a second-hand Porsche and a Volkswagen; wife drives the Volkswagen. Also own yacht and interest in ski chalet. *Major status needs here!*
11.	*Significant other.*	Wife a nurse, four years his senior. Daughter of blue-collar parents. *Has married his nurturing mother and sisters!*
12.	*Golden Spur.*	*Unconscious need to prove manhood by attaining special status, and becoming conspicuously financially independent, thereby outshining the father.*
13.	*Winner or Loser?*	Self-described "winner." *Not in a winning situation at the moment.* Blames current employers for "holding me back." Says he needs some "breaks." *Employer seems to have given him every chance. Has already had a lot of breaks. Likely to end up a loser.*

INTERPRETATION

The cars, yacht, and ski chalet evidence a key need for status, closely followed by money, affiliation, and autonomy—the need cluster of the immature Dominant Dependent.

An indulged upbringing can be reasonably inferred from Lesley's placing as only boy and youngest child in a family of nurturing females. It does not seem surprising that he has married a nurturing spouse several years his senior.

The tough-guy, aggressive management style is consistent with the overall style of the immature Dominant Dependent. The choice of sales career is congruent with natural boyish charm and manipulative ability. It seems likely that Lesley was a strong salesperson who got overpromoted into a marketing manager's role.

Despite the winning facade, Lesley blames others for his failures and seeks to make a "new start" by emigrating. It seems likely that he is suffering from burnout, and unconsciously seeking to flee his on-the-job problems and emotional dependencies.

FLESHING OUT A PORTRAIT

Now that we have some kind of picture of Lesley's overall style, let's go back to the answers to the interview questions, and fine-tune our interpretations to flesh out the profile in terms of the crucial "Will-do" qualities.

Goals.   The Nine Key Concepts

1.	*Observed needs*	Status, money, affiliation, autonomy.
2.	*Prime parental directive*	Be a man.
3.	*Criteria of success*	To become financially independent and successfully self-employed.
4.	*Lifestyle expectation*	Comfortable professional classes.

5. *Central life interest*   Pursuit of sales commissions to maintain an expensive financial comfort level.

6. *Golden Spur*   Compulsion to deny overdependency by proving himself a conspicuous "winner," as evidenced by the acquisition of expensive status-conferring objects and pursuits.

7. *Likely culminating achievement*   Establishing a viable business.

8. *Financial comfort level*   Very high.

9. *Stage in life*   Approaching failure; seeking to flee it.

Work Habits. *Industry, perseverance, self-reliance, orderliness, and job stability*

Lesley seems driven by the voice of conscience. He shows a stable work history, works regular hours, and entertains clients in his spare time. Father appears to have instilled the need to plan, perhaps because he could see that Lesley might otherwise not apply himself. Lesley is also compelled to work hard to maintain his high financial comfort level and status needs. Self-reliance is unlikely to be his strong suit, and we might wonder how much of Lesley's apparent success was due to the efforts of his boss, who quit to go elsewhere. In all, however, a fairly good worker.

People Skills. *Empathy, loyalty, social dominance, and tact. Demonstrated ability to get on and communicate effectively with superiors, peers, subordinates, and clients*

Lesley possesses empathy, loyalty, and tact. He can also turn on the charm to win his way in a one-on-one discussion. He probably has a lot of friends.

He can be socially dominant, but in fact this runs counter to his upbringing and personality, placing him under pressure. A line job will exacerbate that pressure, and significantly impair his ability to check his temper.

He likes the boss to stay out of his hair, and this conscious wish for autonomy almost certainly conflicts with his underlying need for emotional support and guidance. Thus, his general ambivalence and resentment of the firm is not too surprising. He says he is a democratic manager, and this is somewhat in keeping with his need to be liked and admired, and the associated fear of rejection. However, since his employer now seems to have bumped him from the "fast" track and blocked his promotion, we assume the company judges him to lack any further management ability.

Intellectual Ability.   *Reasoning ability. Common sense or judgment. Imagination and creativity*

Lesley's university education, hi-tech leaning, and good grades suggest strong reasoning abilities. His status needs and apparent inability to face reality imply a judgment impaired by wishful thinking. His overdependency will almost certainly impair his ability to make clearheaded decisions and act in accordance with them. His interest in creative pursuits suggests some creative capabilities.

Emotional Adjustment.   *The absence of immature thought processes and behavior patterns. The absence of counterproductive neuroses*

Lesley's upbringing, lifestyle, goals, and presentation all reflect signs of immaturity. His competence seems most likely to be impaired by his dependency needs, his tendency to wishful thinking, his unrealistic goals, and his need to blame others for his current predicament.

Even though he nurses himself, Lesley's health seems to be suffering. The eczema, mild migraines, and indigestion are all almost certainly stress-induced, and the regular daily alcohol intake—which he has probably understated—reflects difficulty in dealing with pressure. In all, it does not seem surprising that Lesley is seeking to flee his problems, and move off in search of fame and fortune in another country.

EVALUATION SUMMARY: LESLEY HARTFORD

STYLE	DOMINANT DEPENDENT
STAGE IN LIFE	Nearing early midlife. Some signs of burnout
Winner/Loser/At-Leaster	Loser/At-Leaster
Goals	
The psychic contract	Prove manhood, independence
The culminating achievement	Successful self-employment
Societal needs	Professional middle class
Financial needs	Above $100,000 per annum

	Almost None	Not Much	Some	A Lot
Emotional Needs				
Achievement		X		
Status				X
Power			X	
Autonomy				X
Self-Improvement			X	
Acceptance/Affiliation				
Work Habits				
Industry			X	
Perseverance		X		
Self-reliance	X			
Orderliness		X		
Job stability			X	
People Skills				
Empathy				
Loyalty	X			
Social dominance	X			
Tact			X	
Relationships with:				
Superiors Mixed				
Peers Mixed				
Subordinates Mixed				
Clients Strong				
Intellectual Dimensions				
Reasoning ability			X	
Judgment	X			
Imagination and creativity			X	
Emotional Adjustment				
Key Indices of immaturity:				
Emotional dependency			X	
Wishful thinking			X	
Disregard for consequences			X	
Ill-disciplined			X	
Overconformism	X			
Showoff tendencies			X	
Pleasure-mindedness			X	
Destructive tendencies		X		

REACHING A FINAL JUDGMENT

So, now you know a *lot* about your subject. Now, finally, you must make a decision: Will you appoint or reject this person to a senior role in your organization? Is there anything else to keep in mind as you weigh this decision? Yes!

Look for Needs within the Subject That Will Be Satisfied on Your Job.   You can lead a horse to water but it will only drink if it is thirsty. Make sure that your job will ease—but not quench—a need or goal that is crucial to the subject *and that is not already being satisfied off the job.* Hiring a money-hungry salesperson to work on commission is often a smart thing to do. If the subject is about to come into a rich legacy, however, then the drive to go on winning sales may be stemmed.

The best sort of need to look for is something that can channel underlying motivations of which subjects themselves may be unconscious. Thus, narcissistic people are often likely to give their best performances in highly visible roles. People who become outstanding successes in any field usually do so because the profession or role that they choose satisfies deep longings instilled in childhood. Thus, the son of *Penthouse*'s publisher made good on his psychic contract—and moved up the social ladder—by founding his own magazine, *Spin,* catering to the musical interests of his generation; the father of Chrysler chief Lee Iacocca at one time owned a fleet of rental cars; and, often, big company minions are attracted to the corporate world because they were raised to value security and conformism.

Discount the Patter of the Subject.   Often a person wants the status and money of a senior job so badly that she overestimates her capacities and persuades an unwitting employer to go along with this lack of realism. An employer will often rationalize such a mistake, saying, "The subject really wanted the job, so I figured she'd be able to handle it." What a non sequitur! Such an employer confuses desire with competence. Wanting to hit a golf ball straight, true, and long—and believing in your ability to do so—is not the same as doing it. The golf ball itself couldn't give a damn how much you believe in yourself, or how far you want to hit it—it responds only to the speed and direction imparted by the clubhead.

Don't Be Swayed by Mere Technical Competence.   Amateur recruiters almost always fall into the trap of overvaluing technical competence. They think that because a subject is knowledgeable and experienced in a chosen field, this will somehow compensate for any emotional deficiencies. This is seldom ever so. Savvy, well-adjusted people can quickly pick up technical skills. But injecting emotional balance, savvy, or leadership ability into mere technicians is virtually impossible.

Don't Overvalue Prior Successes.   A dictum in hiring is that the best guide to future performance is past performance. There is a lot of truth in this, and to be sure, losing habits usually repeat themselves. However, it is a *big* mistake to assume that past successes will also repeat themselves. Indeed, the Greeks had a word for this assumption—they called it *hubris.* Why, you might ask, would a winner not go on winning? For several reasons:

- Skill is not the same as capacity. Skill in running a small grocery store is not the same as the capacity to manage a whole chain.
- Past successes may have actually impaired the physical ability to go on performing. The spirit might be willing, but the flesh simply too weak. Health problems are a prime index of such problems.
- Past successes may have extinguished the underlying drive. The subject may already have crossed his or her emotional and financial comfort levels, and simply not wish for further triumph. Or, the subject might *wish* to press on, yet be unable to muster the emotional or physical resources—the spirit might be willing, but the flesh weak.
- The new environment might be all wrong. Success in one kind of corporate culture might not readily transfer

to another. As the legendary Bill Bernbach of advertising noted, "I'm amused when other agencies try to hire my people away. They'd have to hire the whole environment. For a flower to blossom, you need the right soil as well as the right seed."

- The presence of a strong or creative boss, may account for much of the subject's apparent successes. Such a superior may have nurtured the subject. Without the boss, the subject may be a loser.

Be Prepared to Modify the Job for Which You Are Considering the Subject. To make a good fit, always change the job—never set out to improve the subject. The chances of your being able to change or improve the subject are practically nil.

Your ability to modify the job, however, is great.

Thus, if your subject lacks people skills, then you'll want to modify the job so that she works pretty much alone. If her judgment is iffy, then you'll want to structure the job to remove the need for the incumbent to make important decisions.

When in Doubt, Reject. You have tried, diligently, to discover the real person. You have found out as much as you can, perhaps as much as anyone could have reasonably hoped to discover. Now, however, after all your efforts, you continue to remain in doubt. Well, think on this: you *still* probably don't know the worst! The subject has been putting his or her best foot forward every step of the way—and, though you may have a few qualms, you have nonetheless probably wanted to believe everything. Even now you want to give the subject the benefit of the doubt, charge ahead, and make the appointment to a very important role, so that you can get on with something else. This is a time to count to ten very slowly, to reflect upon the wisdom of the Roman who said *Caveat emptor,* and to bear in mind that the odds of the subject meeting your higher expectations are remote!

CLOSING THE FILE ON LESLEY HARTFORD

In this case, the recommendation to the client was not to hire Lesley, or, if they were sure they wanted him, to downgrade the role. In fact, the client chose to hire Lesley, reasoning that his understanding of the industry was first rate and that he had a sales record to match. They wisely chose to scale down the original senior marketing vacancy, and appointed Lesley manager of a small sales team. Lesley worked at the role for one year, but was "headhunted" and switched employers, taking a much larger position. Nine months later he was fired. He and a partner some years his senior subsequently persuaded private investors to fund their own business, which ultimately failed.

THE CASE OF THE ORDERLY
MAN IN THE BORDERLESS WORLD

Jeremy Wau (forty-four) did not come by this unusual coupling of names by accident. He was born in Hong Kong, the eldest of four children. His Chinese parents emigrated from the mainland to Hong Kong after World War II. Jeremy's father found a job as a clerk, and rose to office manager. His mother was a full-time homemaker. His siblings became, respectively, an accountant, a schoolteacher, a nurse, and a social worker. Jeremy speaks highly of his parents. He remembers they urged him to "become the best" in whatever he chose.

Jeremy's early schooling was in Hong Kong in a more-British-than-the-British environment and educational system. His favorite subjects were mathematics and science, and his interests included debating, reciting verse, and music. His parents sent him to college in the United States, where he studied science and business. He initially graduated with a bachelor of science degree. His parents paid for the first year. Jeremy earned the rest in part-time jobs. Five years later, working nights, he completed a master's in business administration. At college his interests included photography, music, and auto repair. He was elected president of the International Club.

In all, Jeremy worked for three United States corporations. He began his career with a computer manufacturer. He worked in accounting, then plant manufacturing. Two years after Jeremy joined, the company failed. Jeremy moved to a major manufacturing organization where he handled increasingly responsible marketing roles. After being with the company for fourteen years he was appointed worldwide distribution manager. In the late 1980s the company fell into a recession, and Jeremy was among a group of senior executives who found themselves in "outplacement" programs. He quickly found a new job as divisional manager with another organization. His income rose substantially over the next two years, but the company merged with another and Jeremy was made redundant. At that time he was earning a handsome six-figure annual base salary, plus bonus opportunities.

Jeremy married at age twenty-two. His schoolteacher wife, an American, is the daughter of blue-collar parents. They have three children, all sons, aged twenty, nineteen, and seventeen; the elder two are in college, the youngest at high school. The Waus have owned their current home for nearly ten years. The mortgage is less than one-quarter of the value of the home. They own four cars: a Range Rover, a Triumph TR2, an Alfa Sports, and a Saab. They have a moderate investment in the stock market, and a comfortable net worth. Mr. Wau's spare-time interests include membership of an antique auto club. He also mentions in passing that his parents had been educated and converted to Christianity by American missionaries, that they raised their children as Christians, and that he is a member of the vestry in his local Episcopalian church. He is a non-smoker and an "occasional" drinker. He says he enjoys excellent health.

Other remarks proffered during the course of the interview include:

- *Both of my parents were wonderful, and my father was an amazing man, who made sure we all got great educations. Both of my parents urged me to be the best person that I can be. I've always enjoyed a happy home. My wife and I—she's an American of European decent, by the way—enjoy a wonderful life. She is a great person, and incredibly supportive.*

- *My greatest achievement lay in the consolidation of and cost savings I effected for my second-to-last firm. In ten years I hope to realize most of my potential. If I have a worry, it is that I might become mediocre, so I make a special effort to maintain my skills and knowledge.*

- *People say that I'm very competent, and I certainly try to be much more than merely that. I like to be challenged. I'm an achiever, really. I'd like to realize all of my potential. I look at what has to be done and I set about doing it. I don't work for money. There are more things in life than money. It's nice to live well, but you have to keep these things in perspective, too. If I were to choose some other career I'd like to be an orchestra conductor.*

- *I get on well with everyone. I like people. Let's be honest, I need people to help me if I'm going to be successful. I enjoy directing others. I set high goals and make sure that my subordinates know my expectations. Pressure doesn't unduly bother me. I work out the best way to deal with it, and then do whatever has to be done. I don't like doing things that don't have meaning. And, I can get very frustrated when people don't put forth their best efforts. And there are times when I wish I could achieve so much more. But, what the hell, I'm doing pretty well.*

DEVELOPING A PROFILE OF JEREMY WAU

1. Parental socioeconomic positioning.

Father white collar. Upward-striving, anxious for his children to do well. Mother supportive, nurturing. *Parents have overcome significant obstacles, and appear to want their children to be upwardly mobile.*

2. Place in the family. Sibling socioeconomic positioning.

First-born son. All siblings middle to upper-middle class. *Jeremy will have to work hard to maintain his position as #1 son.*

3. *The psychic contract. The core values. The prime parental directive. The tacit criteria of a successful life. The lifestyle expectation.*	Strong achievement orientation. Upward mobility prized. Urged to earn respect for accomplishment in *"New World." Is probably driven to win respect in the corporate world, and in society generally. Wants to be seen to be an achiever. Less interested in money than in respect and self-worth.*
4. *Emotional climate in the home.*	Speaks highly of his father. Remembers him as an amazing achiever. Speaks highly of his mother. *Will want to work hard and fulfill achievement expectations.*
5. *Education.*	Favored demanding subjects and got excellent grades. Elected to leadership roles. Wide ranging interests. Mostly paid his own way by dint of *hard work. Intelligent, sensitive, creative.*
6. *Stated goals.*	Measures his success in terms of on-the-job achievement. Says he wants to be challenged, to realize full potential . . . to lead an orchestra! Very strong achievement, self improvement, and visibility needs.
7. *Persona and presentation.*	"People say that I'm very competent" . . . "I am an achiever" . . . "There are more things in life than money." *Presents self as well-balanced achiever.*

8.	*Choice of career, and history.*	Attracted to line management roles in major corporations. Practical understanding of machinery and strong marketing flair. *One has to wonder about his having worked for three companies that got into trouble. Was it bad luck, or what?*
9.	*Stated management style.*	Sets high goals. Pushes for results. *Is probably reasonably democratic, but overall his achievement needs will probably outweigh everything else, so that he might seem a little too aggressive.*
10.	*Possessions.*	Owns four cars. Two sports cars, one of them an antique, plus a Range Rover and a Saab. *Some status needs—perhaps even some perfectionistic tendencies–here.*
11.	*Significant other.*	Wife a schoolteacher, daughter of blue-collar parents. Met at American college. *Has probably married an attractive, upwardly mobile individual like himself. Has possibly married into the New World.*
12.	*Golden Spur.*	*Might not his emigration to the United States along with his keen pursuit, embrace, and promulgation of "Western values," religion, lifestyle—even spouse—suggest a deep underlying drive to obliterate the past, and become absorbed into—and win unstinting acceptance within an entirely new world?*

13. *Winner or Loser?*	Not a complainer. Looks forward confidently to the future. Sounds realistic in his expectations. *Almost certainly a Winner.*

INTERPRETATION

The cars, and the interest in appearing before a group, suggest status and visibility needs. There is also ample evidence of the need for acceptance—at home, at work, and at recreation. This first-born son seems anxious to maintain his position in the family, intending to do so by realizing his potential and showing achievement as a line executive within the corporate world. He has been well raised, however, relies on his own efforts, is considerate of others. He is not overly pushy or aggressive, and his style is tempered with some pragmatism. Of special interest is that Jeremy shows the ideal kind of adjustment "problem," being secure within himself, yet also driven by a Golden Spur to prove himself to the world at large.

Careful consideration suggests that Jeremy is a pragmatist whose management style, though fairly direct, will vary according to the situation in which he finds himself. So, for the purpose of our model, we have to classify him as an Adult—and it therefore seems likely that his "between-job" status stems from mere bad luck.

FLESHING OUT A PORTRAIT

Goals. The Nine Key Concepts

1.	*Observed needs*	Achievement, self-improvement, acceptance, status.
2.	*Prime parental directive*	Realize your potential and win acceptance in Western culture.
3.	*Criteria of success*	To achieve and win acceptance.

4.	*Lifestyle expectation*	Corporate collegial.
5.	*Central life interest*	Self-realization and acceptance within the corporate world. Specifically, and the *New World* generally.
6.	*Golden Spur*	To retire the past, and, by demonstrating outstanding achievement, attain success, acceptance and personal growth in a new culture.
7.	*Likely culminating achievement*	Corporate chief executive.
8.	*Financial comfort level*	Moderately high. Likes to live in some style. Has three children to put through college, and four attractive cars to maintain.
9.	*Stage in life*	Approaching the winning line.

Work and Habits: *Industry, perseverance, self-reliance, orderliness, and job stability*

Driven by the voice of conscience, a hard worker. Good planning skills. Self-reliant. Likely to be a smart worker. Stable job history.

People Skills: *Empathy, loyalty, social dominance, and tact. Demonstrated ability to get on with superiors, peers, subordinates, and clients*

Possesses empathy, loyalty, and tact. Wants to impress and be remembered. A team player for whom acceptance is important. Is naturally dominant, but tempers this with common sense and great courtesy. Anxious to please his superiors. Will push his subordinates very hard to get results. Is not autocratic, but people will be conscious of his fairly insistent presence.

EVALUATION SUMMARY: JEREMY WAU

STYLE	ADULT

STAGE IN LIFE
Winner/Loser/At-Leaster

WINNER
Approaching

Goals
The psychic contract — Adopt Western corporate business values, achieve and win acceptance in "New World"

The culminating achievement — Corporate chief
Societal needs — Upper collegial corporate
Financial needs — Upper corporate collegial

	Almost None	Not Much	Some	A Lot
Emotional Needs				
Achievement				X
Status			X	
Power1			X	
Self-Improvement				X
Acceptance/Affiliation			X	
Work Habits				
Industry				X
Perseverance			X	
Self-reliance		X		
Orderliness			X	
Job stability				X
People Skills				
Empathy				X
Loyalty				X
Social dominance			X	
Tact				X
Relationships with:				
Superiors Strong				
Peers Strong				
Subordinates Strong				
Clients Strong				
Intellectual Dimensions				
Reasoning ability			X	
Judgment			X	
Imagination and creativity			X	
Emotional Adjustment				
Key indices of immaturity:				
Emotional dependency		X		
Wishful thinking	X			
Disregard for consequences	X			
Ill-disciplined	X			
Overconformism	X			
Showoff tendencies		X		
Pleasure-mindedness		X		
Destructive tendencies	X			

Intellectual Ability: *Reasoning ability. Common sense or judgment. Imagination and creativity*

Interest in mathematics and science suggests strong reasoning ability. Ability to rise with all employers suggests basic good judgment, as does sound financial situation. Interests in photography, antique cars, and verse recital suggest sensitivity and useful creative potentialities.

Emotional Adjustment: *The absence of immature thought processes and behavior patterns. The absence of counterproductive neuroses*

Enjoyed a sound, happy, productive upbringing. Spurred to show great accomplishment. No health problems, and no major hang-ups, though this level of drive might suggest some perfectionistic tendencies.

COMPLETING THE FILE ON JEREMY WAU

Jeremy was placed into an important line management role, proved an outstanding performer, and is in line to lead a major operation.

See the following pages for checklist for Five Common Obstacles to Gathering Information You Need, and for the Ten Commandments for a Good Interview.

FIVE COMMON OBSTACLES TO GATHERING THE INFORMATION YOU NEED

"I have answered three questions, and that is enough,"
Said his father; "don't give yourself airs!
Do you think I can listen all day to such stuff?
Be off, or I'll kick you downstairs!"
LEWIS CARROLL, *ALICE'S ADVENTURES IN WONDERLAND*

Collecting the necessary information looks like a pretty simple task. In fact, it is usually a deceptively complex matter, for many reasons.

1. As an employer, you must often perform two often conflicting tasks: *sizing up* the candidate, and *persuading* him or her to accept a somewhat dicey—if highly rewarding—appointment. Since it is close to impossible to alienate and persuade at the same time, you often just skip asking the kind of hard-nosed or indelicate questions to which you must have answers to make a truly informed decision, out of fear that these queries might somehow offend.

2. Inferior candidates often realize that informed employers would not appoint them to executive roles if their full history were revealed. With the help of outplacement counselors, these candidates often rehearse highly plausible answers to standard interview questions that might otherwise reveal glitches—or godawful problems—in their past employment. They also usually attempt to steer the conversation away from *any* subject—such as health or finances—that might place them in a bad light.

3. In the United States, the equal opportunity laws have rendered many employers wary of attempting to gather some quite crucial—and entirely legitimate—pieces of information.

4. In a litigious culture, whenever you reject anyone, you risk being sued by someone who imagines they have been the victim of some kind of discrimination or invasion of privacy—or who can be persuaded by a hungry

lawyer to mount a baseless case against you merely in the hope of winning some kind of settlement.

5. Time pressures seem to operate against you. You have a vacancy that simply must be filled yesterday! You want to make an appointment and, suddenly, you see someone who looks so great that you feel in your heart there is no need to drag out the screening process. Now, of course, the Syndrome of the Romantic Rush to Judgment comes into play . . .

It is both easier and more difficult to discover the things you need to know when the subject is already working with you. It is easier because you can verify the presence of crucial executive behaviors. And you can arrange to take the subject out to lunch or dinner—in the presence or absence of his or her significant other—and get a good discussion going, perhaps, which might last long into the evening. It is more difficult, however, because social conventions mitigate your ability to explore such factors as dates of past employment, reasons for leaving, salary history, and so on.

TEN COMMANDMENTS FOR A GOOD INTERVIEW

The Master said of him, "His conversation is sound one may grant. But whether he is indeed a true gentleman or merely one who adopts outward airs of solemnity, it is not so easy to say."
THE ANALECTS OF CONFUCIUS

The key to getting anyone to open up to you is to establish a non-threatening atmosphere and environment, along with an easy, apparently laid-back attitude and tone. Most questions, however personal they might seem, are actually fair game for someone aspiring to an executive role. Ideally, however, you want the subject to *proffer* the precise information you need on his or her own volition, with little or no prodding from you. It is neither unethical nor illegal to hear and remember such information. In order to start and keep a subject talking, I suggest the following:

1. *Establish a good environment.* Take no phone calls. Don't permit interruptions. Avoid unnecessary formality. Don't conduct an interview across a desk. I might just say that I was quite amazed at the wealth of extra information candidates offered me after my offices were moved from Rockefeller Plaza into the apparently more relaxed setting of an East 60s four-story Manhattan townhouse.

2. *Establish good rapport in the first few minutes of the discussion.* Don't start your information-gathering if the subject is still defensive or uptight. Make light conversation until the subject relaxes. Everybody pays lip service to this idea, but really smart people *do it.* Your aim is have the subject feel like a participant in a discussion rather than the victim of an interrogation—even though the latter might sometimes be more accurate.

3. *Never show disapproval of any response.* Everything the subject tells you is incredibly interesting. If you don't know what to say, nod your head, smile, and/or emit a friendly grunt.

4. *Get—and keep—the subject talking.* You will learn from the subject's lips rather than from your own. Unless you have unlimited time, resist the temptation to expand at length about yourself or your organization. Many people do this in a misguided attempt to flatter the subject. If flattery is needed, then *flatter by listening.* Pay rapt attention. Hang on every word.

5. *Stay on track.* Make sure you find out what you need to know. Keep a note of the areas you have to cover in front of you, where you can see it, and make sure you hit every item. Don't feel bound to cover everything in one particular order. Sometimes you can get a lot of very useful information by letting the subject bounce around on several issues. But, finally, drag your quarry back to the key items, until you're satisfied that you have uncovered the information you need.

6. *Make notes during the interview.* Words evaporate if not trapped in ink. Don't rely on your memory. Catch the flavor of the language, too. This will later help you to

identify the subject's overall personality style. Contrary to popular opinion, making notes during a conversation will usually encourage a subject to open up and say even more—as any reporter will tell you. Indeed, if you could find a way to interview your subjects in front of a television camera, they'd probably spill *everything.* (I do not necessarily suggest taking notes in the course of a "discussion" with an existing colleague, however, for the conventions are different.)

7. *Never call the subject a liar.* If you think you're not being told the truth, then restate your understanding of the interviewee's position, and seek confirmation. If the apparent untruth is repeated, then check the facts again. If you *have* been told a falsehood, then, usually, it will be just as well to let the matter pass. But don't hire these dissemblers. Not just because they're strangers to the truth, for we might all tell lies if forced to do so, and, after all, salespeople routinely spin a little puffery. No, the real problem here is that your subject has shown poor judgment, *and then repeated it.* In this situation the subject's role was to win your trust by laying all cards on the table—especially when called upon to do so. Could you ever trust a colleague whom you knew attempted to deceive you—twice—during your first meeting?

8. *Begin any discussion by probing the areas of employment and education.* Everybody expects to be asked about these subjects, so you can ask virtually any question. Don't worry if the subject goes off in other directions, you can bring the conversation round later. (This advice might not necessarily hold good for the existing colleague, of course.)

9. *End the interview when you have enough information to make an intelligent rejection.* Most of the time, a thorough probing of employment, education, and health will provide reason enough to reject a subject. Chronic troublemakers, and assorted unemployables, can usually be spotted fairly quickly. If you have already decided to make a rejection, further discussion is redundant.

10. *End every interview on a high note.* Never let a subject feel that you may have already made up your mind not to hire or promote. Best always to build some goodwill.

A client of mine relates the story of being interviewed as a candidate for an important job and treated in an offhand manner. Fifteen years later, the tables were turned. The discourteous interviewer fell upon difficult days and finally found himself applying for a senior role with the huge company that my client had assembled during that time. And now my client was conducting the interview. Both had forgotten all about their earlier encounter—until, suddenly, they recognized each other across the desk!

PART TWO

HOW

TO BE

A

GREAT

EXECUTIVE

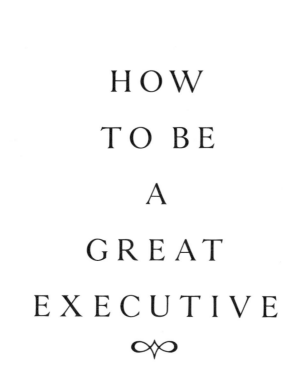

The master said, There are shoots whose lot it is to spring up but never to flower; others whose lot it is to flower, but never bear fruit.

THE ANALECTS OF CONFUCIUS

6

THE
FIVE STEPS
TO TRULY REMARKABLE
SUCCESS

*Some are born great, some achieve greatness, and some
have greatness thrust upon them.*

SHAKESPEARE

A friend of mine, a surgeon, tells of a dictum favored by his colleagues: "Perfect is the enemy of good." In other words, the way to become great—whether as a surgeon or an executive, or anything else—is not to set out to become perfect but instead to aim to be *effective*—all of the time. Soon enough, people will be calling you great, and considering you for higher and higher things. Indeed, some day you'll probably find yourself sitting opposite someone like me, some kind of guru retained by a corporate client to discover just how good you really are!

Suppose for one wild moment that you really were referred to someone for evaluation. What might they be looking for? My own answer is simple. I'd set out to rate you according to my fivefold grading:

- First, what are your *overall goals?* Might you have a special underlying *burning desire?* Will you be able to meet your goals by working with my client?
- Second, do you *work* hard enough—and effectively enough—to achieve your goals?
- Third, do you have the necessary *people skills* to function as a true executive? Do you get on with your boss and peers. Can you lead? Can you deal effectively with clients?
- Fourth, do you have the overall *intelligence* to win your goals?
- And finally, fifth, are you *emotionally well adjusted?* Or are there *incapacitating hang-ups that might get between you and your goals?*

No mystery in any of that. Just good common sense. Yet it took me a lifetime of working with people to make it seem so simple. Let's look a little more closely.

OVERALL GOALS

> *In the long run, men only hit what*
> *they aim at.*
> HENRY DAVID THOREAU

To be a great executive you have to become a great person, and the way to do this is to follow your own personal goals—not somebody else's. Hence: the wisdom of Polonius's advice to his son, "This above all to thine own self be true,/And it must follow, as the night the day,/Thou canst not then be false to any man." Here's a five-step formula to help you onto the right track.

DISCOVER YOUR PSYCHIC CONTRACT

"Know thyself," said the Delphic Oracle. Unfortunately, she didn't say how to do it. For openers, I suggest completing the following sentences:

1. My parents always told me I should _____.
2. The best measure of personal success is _____.
3. The main driving force in my life is _____.
4. I will know for sure that I'm successful on the day that I _____.
5. Realistically, to enjoy a satisfactory lifestyle, I need an annual income of $ _____.

Don't read on yet! Take two or three minutes and finish the sentences. Now, see what you may have discovered.

Response 1   is your *prime parental injunction.* It is the centerpiece of your conscience.

Response 2   is your *guiding criteria of success.* It probably shows a relationship to Response 1—even though you may have left home many, many years ago!

Response 3   reveals your *central life interest,* the activity that takes up most of your thought and energy. This probably relates to Responses 1 and 2.

Response 4   is likely to reveal your *culminating achievement.* If you attain this, you will be a winner in terms of your psychic contract.

Response 5   is your *financial comfort level.* It relates to the *lifestyle expectation* you were programmed to pursue.

This apparently simple approach in fact is very profound. The responses are *your* responses, culled from *your* unconscious, and research shows that the first response is likely to be just as meaningful—and often more meaningful—than any other. Still, it won't do you any harm to turn the sentences and responses over in your mind later, either.

IDENTIFY YOUR OVERALL PERSONALITY STYLE

You might be able to accomplish this fairly quickly merely by contemplating your place in the family, and completing the following sentences:

1. The way I get results is to _____.
2. When I give orders, I _____.
3. After I tell them twice, I _____.

These sentences can be answered in many ways, but as a very quick rule of thumb,
Dominant people say:

1. The way I get results is to press.
2. When I give orders, I expect them to be obeyed.
3. After I tell them twice, I get punitive.

Detached people say:

1. The way I get results is to work to a strategy.
2. When I give orders, I make sure they're clear.
3. After I tell them twice, I look for the cause of the problem.

Dependent people say:

1. The way I get results is to involve people.
2. When I give orders, they don't sound like orders.
3. After I tell them twice, I see if I can help.

Take a look at your responses; they're probably something of a mixture, but you should still be able to discern a pattern.

Anyway, here's the point: You can temper your style, but you can't radically alter it. Therefore, you should come to terms with it.

If you are naturally Dominant, then a job directing others will hold a lot of appeal, and be a good fit. But you should guard against your autocratic tendencies.

If you are Detached, you'll want to find a job that uses your intellectual—and perhaps creative—leanings.

If you are fundamentally Dependent, you may want seriously to ask yourself whether you wish to try to go against the emotional grain by taking on a role that calls for you to have to assert yourself on a daily basis. Better, perhaps to be in a people role, where your good nature can be appreciated and appropriately rewarded. If you still want to press on, however, then do so. Bear in mind, however, that your success or failure will likely hinge upon your capacity to gather other savvy, switched-on subordinates about you.

IDENTIFY THE THINGS YOU OUGHT
TO BE DOING TO SATISFY YOUR INNER SELF

This is no easy task, but a good place to start is by completing the following sentences:

1. I am happiest and most satisfied when I _____.
2. If I could instantly re-educate myself and choose any career, I would be a _____ because
_____.

Both responses seek to identify the special quality searching for expression that comprises your true self. If you are lucky, you already gain maximum pleasure in your present job and role. If so, you are one of the fortunate people. Perhaps you had wise parents, who set you onto the right track early in your life—by not overprogramming you. In fact, this seldom happens for, as Henry David Thoreau noted, "Most people live lives of quiet desperation." If you fall within this latter category, now might be a good time to start looking out for yourself.

FOLLOW YOUR INNER SELF

Most people mistakenly follow the voice of conscience when they should be listening to the voice of their own *selves*. Emerson called this voice the "inner gleam" and wrote:

> *A man should learn to watch that gleam of light which flashes across his mind from within, more than the lustre of the firmament, of bards and sages. Yet he dismisses without notice his thought, because it is his. In every work of genius we recognize our own thoughts; they come back to us with a certain alienated majesty. Great works of art have no more abiding lesson for us than this. They teach us to abide by our own spontaneous impression with good-natured inflexibility when the whole cry of voices is on the other side.*

Remember, it is more important to follow the inner gleam in the big things than in the small things. The "housekeeping" of life—working out what route to take to get to work, when to schedule servicing on the car, and so on—can be handled consciously. But life's big decisions— whom to marry, what vocation to pursue—are best handled by the inner gleam. Most people get all this upside down. They trust the inner gleam on the small things, and mistakenly worry and fret over the big things. They're like the tennis player who tries to control the big points and ends up "choking" instead. The champion just goes ahead and does it, *without fretting!*

SET NEW GOALS AND MAKE
REAL CHANGES IN YOUR LIFE

Following the inner gleam means having the courage to make real changes in your life. This is not easy. You may have to modify your financial and lifestyle expectations in order to pursue your ideal goals—but that might ultimately prove more palatable than your current value system even permits you to contemplate!

If you still want to be an executive.

Since the promise of this book was to help you become a great executive, let's now work on the assumption that you have given your life a lot of thought and you still want to know how to be a great executive. Okay, then, if that's the case, your prime goals should be for achievement and self-improvement. Not power, not status, not security, not service to others or acceptance. No, *achievement and self-improvement*—then everything else will follow. Let me offer three hints for setting your achievement goals:

1. *Set a big—but not unrealistic—*overall dream. Something important to you. It is easier and much more fun to work toward a big idea than a small idea. Remember, too, the advice of Confucius: "The knight of the Way who thinks only of sitting quietly at home is not worthy to be called a knight."
2. *Break your goal up into bite-sized chunks,* and set some *realistic deadlines.* If you don't work to realistic goals, you can quickly become discouraged. Keep your dream in mind, but focus on accomplishing the more immediate tasks, one at a time.
3. *Don't fret about being promoted to manager, or maintaining your economic security.* Keep working toward your achievement needs, steadily and purposefully. Let your achievements win your ultimate promotion.

WORK HABITS

*It is not enough to have great
qualities; we should also have the
management of them.*
LA ROCHEFOUCAULD

I presume we're agreed on the values of industry, perseverance, self-reliance, orderliness. But, as a practical matter,
let me now add this:

*It is better—more fun, less tiring, more productive—to be a smart
and effective worker, than merely a hard worker.*

The trouble with the "makework" mentality is that it
often fails to focus on results. I remember being horrified
many years ago when I worked as an auditor and had to
account for every quarter hour of the day, so they all could
be billed to a client. I subsequently vowed never to work on
an hourly rate, reasoning that I'd rather be paid for output
than time.

The smart thing, then, is to consider integrating the
elements that will permit you to be a great—yet apparently
effortless—producer. Those elements are:

- Achievement needs.
- A burning desire to excel in a particular industry or
  function.
- The voice of a "work-ethic" conscience.
- A high energy level.
- "Smart" work habits.
- A willingness to set realistic deadlines and work steadily
  toward them.

Achievement and Self-improvement Needs.   Great executives always display strong achievement and self-improvement needs. If you don't have such needs, then I doubt
you'll ever be great. You can stimulate these needs, however, by:

Reading the stories of great people.   Such texts reveal that
extraordinary people are for the most part much the

same as you and I. When we realize this, we can feel spurred to emulate them.

Contemplating what you might like from life in the way of material rewards.   Want to own a yacht or a waterfront home, or a master painting to hang in it? Then go get the catalogues, and study them. Pick out your ideal home, yacht, painting, or whatever. Go somewhere to look at it—ideally to touch it—if you can. Think about how it will be when you actually own—and *use*—this thing. Now, reflect upon what service you will offer the world, that might provide the wherewithal to capture that sweet object of your desire. The fact is that ownership of the thing is probably not out of your reach. If it really were, then you probably wouldn't be hankering after it in the first place. So, now is the time to fix your goals, devise your strategy, and go for it! But first, a caveat: *Make sure you really do want the thing you think you really want!*
You might remember Buddha's first three noble truths:

1. Suffering is the condition of mankind.
2. The cause of suffering is desire.
3. To ease the suffering we must rid the desire.

Buddha notwithstanding, it mightn't be much of a world without desire, for as the poet said, "Ah, but a man's reach should exceed his grasp, or what's a heaven for?" A much more useful idea to keep in mind is that *infantile* desire—desire predicated upon essentially childish impulses and delusions not yet outgrown—is the cause of needless suffering. Often, it is only the pursuit and fulfillment of a desire that can rid us of its spell. I once hankered to own an oceangoing racing yacht. When I bought it, I found myself in for a lot of hard work, heartache, and seasickness. I raced it with considerable success (ultimately!) and it was fun to win. Finally, however, I realized that I had the most fun sailing with family and friends, so I sold the yacht. Now, when we feel like going on a sailing holiday, we charter and go bareboat. So, I didn't really want to *own* a yacht, I just wanted to go sailing. Nobody could have told me that, of course; I had to find it out for myself. Striving to acquire material possessions can be very worthwhile, if only to discover in the best Ecclesiastical tradition that almost all is vanity, and that many of life's most-sought-after prizes turn out to be illusory.

Setting a series of life challenges. You might get enthused about painting a portrait, writing a book, climbing a mountain, living in a foreign country, going on a major sea voyage, perhaps even taking a ride on the New York subway system. Any of these challenges will expand you and make you a better person—and therefore a better executive.

Setting a series of goals for your business life. This is the direct route to success. What will you do? Get an MBA or a doctorate? Not a bad place to begin, but a lot of very successful executives don't have either, of course. Often, it's much better to begin with a quantifiable project: installing a computer system, developing an invention, or bringing in a lot of new business.

Developing a special expertise. It can be very smart to develop a talent—or acquire one. I was nearly forty years old when I suddenly realized the feasibility of becoming an international authority in the analysis of the incomplete sentence blank, a form of psychological questionnaire favored by sophisticated psychologists. I immediately bought a computer and hired a programmer to help me set about the task. It turned out to be much greater than I'd ever appreciated, but it also turned out to be a very wise decision. Quite apart from any commercial value, the honing of such an expertise promotes inner confidence.

Developing a Burning Desire. As Alfred Adler was the first to point out, a burning desire—or magnificent obsession—usually springs from an unconscious underlying drive to compensate for some real or imagined inner shortcoming. Thus, beautiful models often feel very plain, achievers often feel like impostors, and psychiatrists often doubt their own sanity—showing the highest suicide rate of any profession! The best kind of burning desire is the desire to realize your own special self and talents.

The Work-Ethic Conscience.   By all means feel free to hire people who are driven by the voice of conscience—but don't be unduly badgered by your own. If you find that you fall into the category of those lucky/unlucky souls who cannot rest when there is work to be done, then make a conscious effort to maintain an overview of your life and *delegate.* If you are not driven by a work-ethic conscience, then your life will be more fun, but you may have to make a greater effort to maintain the focus on your goals. In fact, many very creative and effective entrepreneurs are pulled along by their own achievement needs, rather than driven by the voice of conscience.

A High Energy Level.   It used to be that executives were always tired. Now, a whole generation has discovered that energy level is related to aerobic exercise and diet. Health clubs have become shrines to the new religion of Fitness, and the wine of our forefathers has been forsaken for the holy waters of Perrier, Poland Spring, and Pelligrini. Better jump on the bandwagon, or get left behind. If you're serious about your life:

- Get 30 to 45 minutes of aerobic exercise three times a week. Running is good, but some kind of game is a great supplement, for as Goethe said, "Man is fully man only when he plays."
- Consider working out with weights to maintain your upper body—also one of the best ways to control a paunch! Don't go overboard on this, just keep yourself toned. About 10 minutes a session two or three times a week ought to do it.
- Cut back drastically on most meats and animal fats.
- Limit your intake of alcohol, ideally to evenings when you don't have to go to work next morning.
- Don't smoke! A survey of my own firm's files revealed that less than 3 percent of senior North American executives smoke cigarettes. Not surprising, really.

I speak with the passion of a reformed sinner on this subject, for in my early thirties I didn't bother to take care of myself and finally got sick from work and wine, food and fatigue. I remember lying on my sickbed and wondering how I could have been so silly. I made a vow right then and there to make amends to my body, and slowly but surely I did. I'm not obsessive about fitness, of course, but I do take care, nonetheless.

"Smart" Work Habits. Working smart is about getting maximum results from apparently minimum efforts. The people who can do this usually pay great attention to the following elements:

- *An overriding concern with results.* It's not the hours you put in, it's the work you put in the hours. Results and time are intrinsically related, but I personally focus on results obtained, not minutes lost.
- *Plan for getting where you want to go.* You've already defined a dream and broken it into bite-sized chunks. Now, break those chunks into spells of 90 minutes or so each, and insert them one a day, or so, into your work schedule. Why 90 minutes, you might ask? *Because it's an effective and do-able unit.* You can't accomplish much in less, and concentration can wander after an hour and a half. Better to set yourself a task that will take an hour and a half and *get it done* than do nothing—or get started but complete nothing!
- *Keep a daily "to do" list and finish three items every day.* At the top of your list should be at least one 90-minute item from your most pressing goal. The prolific novelist Anthony Trollope got up in the morning at 4:00 A.M. and wrote 3000 words, then got to his office job—he was a very successful civil servant—by 8:00 A.M. Graham Greene, in his autobiography *A Sort of Life,* said that he set himself the task of writing 1500 words every day. He counted the words as he went along, and when the magic number was reached he simply laid down his pen. Like most good writers, writing did not come easily to him—but he felt he could manage 1500 words a day. The historian Arnold Toynbee wrote only 250 words a day—yet he still completed his twelve-volume masterpiece: *A Study of History.*
  The second item on your list—every second day, any-

way—should be an item that you regard as *important yet not urgent.* If you don't make a special effort to give such items priority, then you might never get around to doing them at all. If you're a compulsive worker, don't forget to include family and personal items under this rubric. The latter two items on your list needn't take 90 minutes each, of course. But whatever you put there, complete it.

- *Reward yourself for your successes.* Schedule coffee breaks and other treats so that they are taken upon completion of each of the items on your "to do" list. Reinforce your own good habits!
- *Nurture your psychic energy.* Psychic energy may be defined as the energy you expend when you concentrate. It takes effort to attain a deep attention span, and this energy is greatly depleted by forced lapses of concentration—*interruptions!* The savvy executive therefore plans his or her day to maximize spells of concentration and minimize interruptions. Three good ways to do this are

> *Establish a "quiet time."* Fix an hour in the day when you will take *no* interruptions. You need time to clear your head, to plan, to get housekeeping out of the way, to handle correspondence, to reflect.
> *Establish a "response time."* Save time and energy by lumping all the time-wasters together and getting them out the way at the same time. Return most of your incoming calls at a fixed hour in the day. You might take an urgent call outside of this time, but aim to handle all lower-priority items in this hour.
> *Work regular hours.* I was once told that the people who rule the world are at their desks at 8:00 A.M. in the morning. Not 6:00 A.M. or 7:00 A.M., for they don't need to overdo it. And not 9:00 A.M., either, for they want some quiet time before plunging into the day. As Schopenhauer said, "Do not shorten the morning by getting up late; look upon it as the quintessence of life, as to a certain extend sacred."
>   Of course, this approach has to be tempered by your own working style for, after all, different peo-

ple work best at different times of the day. However, it is wise, I think, to keep a regular schedule and to ensure that you get enough quiet time.

- *Learn to use a word processor.* A secretary is a wonderful asset, but modern technology has charms all of its own. I have a personal computer, laser jet printer, and fax machine right behind me. I can touch-type and revise a letter faster than virtually any typist, and have it faxed—or mailed—anywhere in the world in about two minutes. I might not always choose to type my own stuff, but I can if I want to—and often do!

- *Organize your desk.* Managing a desk space is a deceptively difficult task that many people never come close to mastering. That space will be in front of you every day of your career, however, so you can either manage it—or you can let it clutter your day, your mind, and your life. For what it's worth, my suggestions—assuming you are right-handed—are to:

  Set yourself up with a desk, in and out trays, filing drawers, left-hand side return, credenza, highlighter, pen, pencil, fax machine, and wastebasket. Position your phone on the desk close to your left hand, leaving your right hand free to write.
  Place your Rolodex or what-have-you next to the phone.
  Keep a three- or five-year diary in the middle of your desk.
  Position the in-tray on the right-hand side of the desk, and the out-tray on the left-hand side of the credenza.
  Install your personal word processor, printer, and fax machine on the side return.
  Keep the books you need in or on the credenza. (I keep mine in a bookcase within easy reach, above the credenza.)
  Don't sort your in-tray correspondence into manila files—out of sight, out of mind! Instead, sort this stuff into clear plastic files—color-coded for priority, if you like—and lay them on the credenza behind you (having highlighted the items that need your attention).

Keep your current files in the filing drawers within reach of your fingertips.

• *Establish effective filing systems.* A muscle is stored energy—and so is a filing system. If you work on your muscles, and use them, you build them up and make them powerful. It's the same with a filing system. A colleague of mine enjoyed the almost awe-inspiring knack of producing virtually any piece of correspondence or information in a matter of seconds. It was a great quality, and helped the fellow to earn a lot of money. I marveled at his secret, until I discovered that his father had been a *librarian!*

If you have a computer bent, you might want to keep your files on your computer. There's a lot to be said for old-fashioned Rolodexes and the like, however. They never go down, and there's usually a piece of paper and a pencil handy. Better to have a usable system than something more sophisticated than you can be bothered to maintain. You'll need files on

> *People.* Keep a Rolodex with the names, phone numbers, and brief (very brief) background of every person you know and meet. The numbers will go out of date, but you'll find a way of getting in touch if need be.
> *Correspondence, etc.* Set up four or more overall files:
>   General correspondence
>   Client correspondence.
>   Must read—then save. Important articles, news, and so on. Read during commute home.
>   May read—then discard. Read on plane journey, maybe.
> *Finances.* These you should keep on computer—or have someone keep for you—because modern accounting packages are marvelous, flexible, and cheap.
> *Time.* Plan—and monitor—your progress in your diary. Keep your "to do" list on top of the diary.

• *Try to handle every piece of paper only once.* You won't always succeed, but this is a wonderful rule of thumb. Read the item, highlight the material that needs action, then decide what to do now:

> Initiate action immediately.
> Action required but further thought or discussion needed. Place behind you on your credenza.
> Interesting or useful: read and save. Place into reading file #1.
> "Must read" file.
> "May read" file. Discard for sure if not read within two weeks.
> File to wastebasket!

- *Be expedient.* Don't stand on ceremony. Don't write unnecessary letters or memos. If possible, highlight the query, write your reply by hand alongside it—and fax the reply immediately. Use the phone if that will be quicker and more effective. Don't send a letter if you can send a fax.
- *Make good use of the wastebasket.* Throw junk away fast. Don't file things you won't need.
- *Train an assistant to do most of the above for you.* A good assistant can handle most of the routine for you.

Set Realistic Deadlines and Work Steadily Toward Them.
The fastest way to get the kinks out of the hose is to turn on the water! Deadlines provide that same kind of pressure. If you don't have any deadlines, you're probably kidding yourself about your overall goals. Remember the words of Goethe:

> *Are you in earnest?*
> *Then begin this minute,*
> *For boldness has power,*
> *And magic in it.*
> *Begin it! Now!*

A deadline says that you are serious about taking on and completing a task. If you set deadlines, you will automatically work with a sense of urgency. The deadline forces you to work even when you don't feel like it. A lot of people put off setting deadlines and wait for the "right mood" to come upon them. In fact, the right mood is something of an illusion. Countless creative people have observed that their moods made virtually no difference in the quality of their output. W. S. Gilbert, of Gilbert & Sullivan fame, said: "If I had waited for the muse to come upon me, I would never have written anything." In fact, the "muse" seldom comes upon anyone until well into the project.

It is important to set *realistic* deadlines, of course. Don't try to do too much, or you may end up disappointed—but keep up a steady pace. Get some momentum up and keep it going!

PEOPLE SKILLS

> *When dealing with people, let us remember that we are not dealing with creatures of logic. We are dealing with creatures of emotion, creatures bustling with prejudices and motivated by pride and vanity.*
> DALE CARNEGIE

Ronald Reagan said that success in life is being able to command a better quality of audience. This funny, insightful remark reveals former President Reagan's realization that the quality of an audience is related to the quality of the performance.

The savvy executive also realizes that his or her success depends upon the ability to get along with an interactive audience of peers, superiors, subordinates, and clients or outsiders. As you'll recall, getting on with these people calls for at least some measure of the four human qualities—empathy, loyalty, social dominance, and tact—and four of the prime communications skills—listening, discussing, writing, and advocating.

In my experience, it is usually quite pointless to attempt to develop an executive's people skills by means of what my late chairman used to call "pious admonitions." Let's consider cognitive therapy instead.

COGNITIVE THERAPY AND PEOPLE SKILLS

Cognitive therapy boils down to helping people re-arrange their thinking. For our purposes here, it means showing someone—and having them fully realize—that it is *smart* to get on with people. Once we realize that, modifying the quirks in our behavior becomes a more straightforward exercise. Let's just look at some items of social intelligence that guide the savvy executive's behavior:

- It is a shrinking world and people meet again more frequently than ever in history, so it is wise to treat *all* people as if we were going to want a crucial, unexpected future favor from them.
- Both enemies and friends virtually always increase their personal power with the passage of time.
- Friendships come and go, but enemies accumulate.
- Good friends often become bitter enemies.
- Present colleagues are likely to be called upon for crucial future favors.
- A former boss is likely to be asked to comment on the competence and personal qualities of his or her subordinates, without their specific awareness.
- It is better to have people rooting for you than against you.
- As a straight psychological fact, people generally treat others as they are treated. Hence the wisdom of the Golden Rule: Do unto others as you would have them do unto you.
- If you treat people well, they will respond in kind.
- If you treat people badly, they will want to get even when the opportunity arises to do so.
- People treat us as we deserve to be treated.
- It is usually unwise to antagonize people.
- It is stupid to antagonize people unnecessarily.
- It is usually pointless to criticize.
- More flies are trapped with honey than with vinegar.
- Words unspoken cause least offense.
- People are creatures of emotion rather than logic.
- People act in their own perceived best interests.
- Most people want to help, and like to be thanked.

- Mature friends and associates are happy for you when you succeed. Immature friends and associates would rather commiserate with you in your failures.
- The best reason to treat people as if they were important is that they are.

For my own part, the thoughts that cross my mind in tricky personal situations are:

- I must have done something to attract the person and situation now facing me.
- If I deal with this situation adroitly, I can build some goodwill.
- Quite apart from what I want here now, I may also want a crucial future favor from this person someday.
- This person will say something about me after we part company.
- Let me try to enlist this person's cooperation and help.
- What does this person really want? How can I address or resolve that need?
- What are the key *issues*?
- What do I want? How can I express my need in terms of the other person's needs?
- How can we work out a deal so that we both get what we want?
- Let's just talk about this quietly and reasonably, and not get polarized.
- If I stay calm and reasonable, my chances of resolving this satisfactorily are highest.
- I can push for a fair resolution without being aggressive.
- If I don't get what I want, I will remain poised—and focus once more on ways to satisfy the other person's needs so that we both get what we want.
- If we can't agree, I can always talk to a superior.
- If in the end I don't get what I want, then I am probably partly to blame, and I should try to make sure I don't get in the same position again.

CONTEMPLATING YOUR OVERALL STYLE AND ADDRESSING YOUR LIKELY PEOPLE PROBLEMS

One of the best ways to improve your people skills is to consider your own personality style, and address the kinds of faults that are intrinsic to each type.

The Dominant. If you are a Dominant, then you probably get what you want a lot of the time. You could do even better, however, if you tried to improve your listening skills—are you hearing me?—and your sensitivity to the needs of others. You have an annoying tendency to be overly certain of your opinions, and to press your views on others. At your worst you are rigid, overbearing, and not much of a friend. You probably have many possessions but few real friends. You probably say you don't care, you might even think you don't care. But you do! With a little effort, life could be much easier and infinitely more rewarding.

The Detached. People admire your ability to strike a middle course and to reach a practical compromise. If you have a problem, it probably stems from overconcern with strategies and plans. You could press a little more for what *you* want instead of always striking the middle ground. You might try to develop the warmer and more outgoing side of your personality. Overall, however, you'll probably work out a way to get what you want from people.

The Dependent. You are a sensitive and (usually) popular person, whose problems as an executive probably stem from your overconcern with winning the acceptance and approval of others. You are so anxious to be accepted that you find it difficult to press for results. When you attempt to assert yourself, you run the risk of overdoing it and losing your temper. You possibly hanker for greater status and power, without quite realizing that those who have it envy your knack for making friends. It will not be easy for you to be a great executive, and in many ways it might not be worth all the effort. Best to reconcile yourself to a role that uses your abundant qualities of empathy and loyalty.

THE BEST ADVICE FOR
DEVELOPING YOUR PEOPLE SKILLS

The best way I know of to develop your people skills is to jump off the deep end and attend a public speaking group. I did this myself many years ago, when I suffered from a crippling stammer. I learned to master my stammer, won many oratory prizes, and later came to be asked to teach public speaking (for I knew all the problems, and could empathize with every anxiety any nervous person ever felt). I never saw any method of improving people skills—or developing confidence—as effective as attendance at a public speaking class. In the space of seven short weeks I saw wallflowers grow into luxuriant plants. I saw pompous people develop humility. I saw veritable explosions of empathy and understanding.

As an executive, you will often be called upon to "say a few words." If you speak untutored, you will almost certainly make many mistakes, for public speaking is a skill that must be acquired and developed. If you don't hone that skill, you'll doubtless unwittingly bore or even offend an audience. If you do seek tutelage, however, you'll probably make a grand job of every public speaking opportunity. So, don't just take my word for it; find a local group, jump in, and don't quit until you feel qualified to:

- Give an impromptu speech on *any* subject.
- Give an instructive lecture.
- Make a persuasive presentation to a group of clients.
- Give an inspiring speech to those whom you aspire to lead.

OVERALL INTELLIGENCE

I dealt regularly with two executives called Simon—Simon Gold and Simon Green. They looked similar, and sounded identical. Both were from the "wrong side of town" and in a big hurry to prove themselves to be outstanding people.

Simon Gold attended one of my management seminars,

and became a good client and friend. He had a Ph.D., and had enjoyed an outstanding academic career before founding a computer software business. He had some great ideas, and recruited some able people. He got into financial trouble, but saved the company by persuading twenty key staff members to work for six months without salary or wages. They believed in him and stayed on. They liked him, but pointed out that he was something of an impractical dreamer—a wonderful person, but too sincere and open to be characterized as an astute businessperson.

Simon Green had been a candidate for a chief executive role. He had a bachelor's degree in business, an outstanding track record as a salesman, and useful experience as a senior sales executive. His résumé proudly listed his prestigious Fifth Avenue address, as well as various *Who's Who* listings. Everyone agreed that Simon Green was really smart—a shrewd, clever operator who could make things happen and always come out on top.

Simon Gold merged his firm with another, got appointed president, and eventually sold out to an even larger firm—which put $15 million into his pocket! Simon Green landed a job as chief executive, ran up some wonderful sales, sold the company to a competitor—and got fired!

Simon Gold founded another computer business, and has so far built the annual sales to $200 million. Simon Green, upon his dismissal, joined a competitor company, pulled in some business for them—and then got fired again!

I was intrigued and followed these cases very closely. It became clear that although people judged Simon Gold to be somewhat naive, they trusted him and put him in charge because they realized he focused on the task at hand—and not merely his own selfish interests. It was the opposite with Simon Green. Everyone agreed that he was smart, and he could sell. They also feared to trust him out of concern that he might ultimately turn his formidable business savvy against them. I can draw at least two morals from this story:

- It takes great cleverness to conceal one's cleverness.
- Too clever is dumb.

Let's move on now, and think a little more about this notion of intelligence.

HOW TO EXPAND YOUR OVERALL INTELLIGENCE

You can make yourself much smarter. The brain is like a muscle: Use it, and it expands. Fail to use it, and it atrophies. When I was growing up, my mother urged me to feed my brain by eating fish. No, Mother, what feeds a brain is *ideas*. Feed yourself enough of these and you'll soon be having wonderful ideas of your own. If you'd like to improve the quality of your own thinking processes, I suggest you try to enhance each of the seven areas that comprise your overall intelligence.

Education. Education is best regarded as a lifelong process. Savvy executives stay abreast of what's happening in their fields. They know that whenever they're not keeping up with what is happening in their industries, someone else out there is, and when it comes time for the client to choose which firm to go with, she'll opt for the best mousetrap available.

Experience. The savvy executive plans his career so that he gets a variety of great experience—experience that will provoke both intellectual and emotional growth. He realizes, too, that important lessons can be learned from every aspect of his job, even the apparently dull and mundane. In my first job I worked in a bank, and was assigned the tasks of refilling the customer inkwells, changing the blotters, and keeping the postage tin and register. I was embarrassed to be ceded these menial roles, until the manager himself, a silver-headed father figure, took me aside.

"Mr. Wareham," he said (I was a very youthful eighteen at the time), "I have assigned you two vital tasks, and I will be looking closely to see how you perform. First, you are charged with the duty of making sure the customer is happy from the moment he walks in the door. You alone can assure this, by permitting him to complete his deposit slips with a clean pen, fresh ink, and a neat blotter. Second, I want you to bear in mind that nothing is more important to any company than to correspond with the client. To this end, you will be my watchdog, for you will make a careful record of all outgoing communications. And, finally, you'll watch over the petty cash with an eagle eye, for, believe it or not, most would-be white criminals begin their careers by pilfering in such places." As you can appreciate, dear reader, I had been charged with awesome duties and primed to learn lessons I never forgot!

Reasoning Ability. The ability to reason is an easily acquired skill, yet I am often surprised and distressed to discover that some otherwise intelligent and able executives lack the ability to hold an idea in train, or to follow a line of argument to its logical conclusion. As a practical matter, every executive would be well advised to complete a formal course in the application of reasoning ability— *logic*—for it is a discipline that is quickly learned and can be applied with great benefit to practically every situation or conversation. If you don't want to do a whole course in the subject, then just go out and buy a popular text.

Judgment. This is a trickier matter. As we've seen, judgment is a function of education, experience, emotional growth, and reasoning. The wider your overall knowledge, the greater your likelihood of calling upon enough prior cases to make a sound judgment in some new area. The key areas in which you need to pay careful attention to your judgment are (a) your business decisions, and (b) your people decisions.

Business decisions. I'll leave it to you to master the knowledge side of the business in which you have chosen to make your career. As far as reaching decisions goes, however, here's the formula I suggest:

- Get as much information on the subject as is feasible. Recognize that it will be impossible to get enough information, and accept that you're going to have to use some intuition.
- Sift it, contemplate it, and sleep on it.
- Establish your boundary conditions—the underlying

criteria that will guide your decision. Recognize that the boundary conditions may be in conflict, and try to make sure that they're not.

- Discuss the decision with people who share your interest in the outcome.
- Make your decision.
- Sleep on it.
- Modify it if necessary.
- Go with it.
- Monitor your progress to make sure the result is to your liking.
- If the decision isn't working out, spot the problem, and fix it. *Make* your decision work.
- Don't be afraid to back out if you got it wrong!

People decisions.   As far as your understanding of people goes, one of the best things you can do—apart from rereading this book—is to make a real effort to read many of the great novels and plays. For, becoming a good judge of people entails being able to feel what they feel—and the writer's art is to evoke these very emotions in you. Shakespeare was onto the ideas Sigmund Freud made famous long before the Viennese professor himself. So were many other authors, of course. If you don't read novels, then at least read some good biographies. If there were a simple, surefire formula for making judgments about people, then horrendous mistakes of hiring and promotion would not be so commonplace. But they are. My own not-so-simple but do-able five-step suggestion is:

1. Read as many novels, plays, and biographies as you can to build your vocabulary of overall styles (within the Dominant/Detached/Dependent framework mentioned).
2. Make a conscious effort to be analytical in reaching any judgment about people. Try to get your subject's entire life history every time.
3. Place greater reliance on performance than intentions.
4. Assume that unhappy quirks, habits, and outcomes will probably repeat themselves, but that past successes might not!

5. If you're in doubt, and have money riding on the outcome, improve your risk-reward ratio by getting a professional outside opinion.

Creativity. Creativity is the capacity to make connections that no one else has ever made. Not very many people can do this. Creative people can often be spotted by a particular trait: they seem wrapped up in their own thoughts, lost in the world of imagination. The reason for their inward introspection is that creativity is a product of the unconscious mind. Creativity must be started, however, by *making a conscious effort to grapple with the problem at hand.*

The rules for developing your creativity are similar to those for making a good decision:

- *Develop a rich imagination.* Feed your mind by attending art exhibitions, attending plays, reading novels, working around your own house—doing, doing, doing. . . .
- *Research your project.* Toss all this material into the hopper of your unconscious.
- *Let your mind lie fallow for a few days.* Do something else, get some exercise, don't fret.
- *Kick-start your unconscious* by sitting down at your desk and trying to come up with a solution. This, frankly, is the hardest part of the exercise, for it is *impossible* to reach a truly creative solution merely by means of conscious effort.
- *Don't quit.* Your first attempts to find solutions will probably be pretty bad and tempt you to think about quitting. Don't do it.
- *Feel your feet leave the ground.* Suddenly, another force takes hold of you. Suddenly, your ideas take wing and all sorts of wonderful things begin to happen. Suddenly, the idea you are seeking comes up out of your unconscious *like an atoll coming up out of the sea.* How can you tell that your idea really is a product of your unconscious? You will know immediately, for your creation will possess *an elegance that you could never have created consciously!*

EMOTIONAL ADJUSTMENT

The first phase in the development of leadership, the first step toward the fast track, is to stop pretending, especially to ourselves, that we are something that we are not. . . .
Own up to our strengths and weaknesses. . . . Accept that we do not always operate at our highest levels. . . . Accept that we are where we are because of the choices we have made in the past. . . . Accept that we do not fully control our destinies . . . live in the present and not the past.
BARBARA A. KOVACH

The key to being a great executive is to have an adjustment problem that spurs your motivation, but does not unduly fetter your abilities.

As mentioned, the most common adjustment problems stem from immaturity and overdependence.

A person may also have suffered problems of childhood abuse or rejection that impair his or her ultimate competence. Harvey P. is a case in point. Harvey was raised in an unhappy home. His parents shared the same property but seldom the same dwelling. The mother, an assertive, thwarted, ambitious nurse, owned the property, and Harry's father, a gentlemanly government servant, was often confined to a shed behind the main house. Whenever Harry spoke to his father, his mother sulked and refused to speak to Harry, often for weeks on end. Though a naturally gregarious and fun-loving person, Harry grew into a secretive and somewhat paranoid adult, for whom mixing with colleagues presented all sorts of problems. Spurred by his mother's ambitions for him, Harry set high goals, but alas, on account of his lack of people skills, was never able to achieve them.

Similarly, Robert R. had suffered a difficult relationship with his father. Finally, all communication broke down. Robert was a person of considerable talent and determination. He had earned several degrees, and his goal was to become self-employed; his security needs deterred him from taking the plunge, however. He joined a small share-broking firm and proved himself an outstanding, consistent, well-organized, industrious broker. Robert deeply resented working for someone else and came to hate both the firm and his boss. Though he performed well, he proved such a dour, complaining, negative influence that his boss ultimately fired him. The same thing happened in his next job. Not until Robert decided to seek psychological counseling did he come to grips with his real problems: the feelings of rejection and anxiety that prevented him from striking out on his own, and his hatred of his father who had so unfairly rejected him.

IMPROVING YOUR
PERFORMANCE UNDER PRESSURE

Let's just take a minute or so and consider how you handle pressure at the moment, by having you pull out your pen and complete the following sentences:

1. When they put me under pressure, I _____.
2. When the competition gets rough, I _____.
3. When they play politics, I _____.
4. What gets me into trouble is _____.

Now, let's consider a few typical responses to the first three of these sentences.

1. When they put me under pressure, I

>   enjoy it
>   don't perform as well
>   work harder
>   work smarter
>   look for a creative way out.

The savviest and best-adjusted executives tend to respond that they enjoy working under pressure, and that they work smarter or more creatively. If you answered that you don't perform as well, or that you simply work harder, then you may be able to effect a significant improvement in your ability to deal with pressure simply by taking time out to come up with a strategy for dealing with it.

2. When the competition gets rough, I

> don't like it
> enjoy the game
> get rough too
> work harder
> work out a way to beat them.

Savvy executives enjoy the game, and devise a strategy for coming out on top. Working harder is a useful but not always productive way to deal with the situation. Getting rough or angry is likely to be *counterproductive* to winning.

3. When they play politics, I

> get upset or disgusted
> play too
> try not to get involved
> steer the conversation back to the job at hand.

Executives who get to the top are usually pretty good politicians. They often respond that they "play too," or that they steer the conversation to where they want it. Staying out of the fray can be useful, but on balance doesn't reflect the same level of confidence in one's advocacy skills. Getting upset or disgusted is not going to be much use to anybody, of course.

Now, go back and look at each of your answers again. Are you happy with what you see? Or would you like to do something about ridding yourself of any unhappy responses? How do I that? you might ask. Well, very simply, by becoming a better-adjusted person.

IMPROVING YOUR LEVEL OF ADJUSTMENT

Most badly adjusted executives, like most people, lack the courage to tackle their emotional problems. They let the unconscious mind take over, and they attempt to deny their problems to themselves and to the world, frequently by setting out to prove that they are "bigshots."

If you are really serious about wanting to deal with your adjustment problems, you must begin with a further authentic self-examination. The first thing to consider is your health. Do you suffer from heart problems, high blood pressure, frequent headaches or migraines, ulcers, or frequent indigestion? Do you smoke or drink more than three times a week? Do you take tranquilizers, or similar medication? Do you have problems sleeping or relaxing? Do you have problems with your weight? Is there anything else about your health that might be causing you concern?

Virtually any health problem suggests that the pressure and stress of your job are imposing undue stress upon your body. You can continue to push yourself, of course, but ultimately you are wasting two valuable resources: (a) your health, and (b) the days of your life.

Next, you might check the list of facesavers to which incompetent executives commonly turn and see if any of them apply to you.

Finally, let's have a really truthful response to that last incomplete sentence:

What get's me into trouble is _____.
Responses to this are all over the lot, but they include
taking on more than I can handle
not listening to others
flying off the handle
being too truthful
shooting from the hip.

Take a good look at your own answer, whatever it might be, because frankly it's probably very accurate and won't require much analysis for you, me, or anyone to spot a fundamental flaw in your makeup or habits—which, if you don't make an effort to deal with, will probably hang around, like a faulty golf swing, for the rest of your life.

Let's assume that you have identified a couple of health problems, or that you have a worry or two about your overall performance, and you're serious about tackling the quirk you just spotted in the gets-me-into-trouble sentence. What should you do now? My suggestion is to adopt a holistic approach, and set about changing many of your attitudes and habits. To do this you should:

Establish a sound base. This was Clausewitz's first principle of war. Buddha expressed a similar thought: "Let the wise man make of himself an island that no flood may overcome." So, too, savvy executives establish the physical, emotional, and material resources to be able to withstand virtually any storm.

Join some form of health club offering a tailored, sophisticated workout program. You could take up jogging, of course, or something similar, but the special virtue of the health club is that a pleasant regimen will be imposed—and reinforced. You'll also meet a lot of nice people like yourself, people who are serious about improving the quality of their lives.

Seek psychological counseling. There is not much point in working on the body without the mind. Best to try to identify the unconscious forces that are pressing you into a corner. If you don't feel that this kind of thing is for you, just bear two points in mind: (1) Since the source of your problems is almost certainly locked in your unconscious, then, in classic Catch-22 tradition, you'll be compelled to deny any need for treatment! (2) Becoming conscious of your problems, and treating them, necessarily involves a *process*—the process of psychoanalysis and psychotherapy. You can't resolve your underlying emotional problems by reading books about them and contemplating them, any more than you can build your body by contemplating the pushups you ought to be doing. Self-help books are great to read, of course, and useful too. But if you want the kind of self-insight that really can make a difference, then get serious.

Rely upon your inner gleam to pull you through. When times get rough and the pressure mounts, it is comforting to know that you can rely upon something greater than merely your conscious mind. In the eye of even the greatest hurricane, there is a place that is perfectly quiet and still. So, too, when our minds are buffeted by unhappy fates and dire circumstances, we can always reach back into the deep quiet place that harbors our own true selves and be guided by the inner gleam. Great executives—no less than great athletes, artists, or composers—know this place very well. They have been there many times before, and know they will go back there again.

We can set our goals, devise our strategies, and give our best efforts. But in the end, as in the beginning, it is the inner gleam that will guide us safely to our proper destination.

APPENDIX

KEY INDICES OF MOTIVATIONS, MATURITY, WORK HABITS, AND PEOPLE SKILLS

The lists below are intended to stimulate the thoughts of the intelligent reader, and to evoke a flavor for the kinds of clues an experienced evaluator might consider—and then sometimes disregard: In some places the lists are intentionally incomplete, for undue specificity might merely mislead or over-stereotype. The following prime needs (and related secondary needs) are listed:

KEY MOTIVATIONS

- Achievement
- Power
- Rationality
- Affiliation
- Autonomy
- Service
- Security
- Status
- Money
- Investigate

APPROXIMATE NEED CLUSTERS
RELATING TO OVERALL PERSONALITY STYLES

Dominant
Power
Status
Income
Achievement

Dominant/Dependent
Mature:
achievement, service, power

Immature:
money, status, affiliation

Dominant/Detached
Mature:
achievement, rationality, power

Immature:
status, power, autonomy

Detached
Rationality
Autonomy
Self-improvement

Detached/Dependent
Mature:
rationality, service

Immature:
security, rationality, status, acceptance

Detached/Dominant
Mature:
achievement, rationality, power

Immature:
status, power, autonomy

Dependent
Affiliation
Service
Approval

Dependent/Dominant
Mature:
achievement, service, power

Immature:
money, status, affiliation

Detached/Dependent
Mature:
rationality, service

Immature:
security, rationality, status, acceptance

PRIME NEED	ACHIEVEMENT
Likely overall style	*Dominant or Detached*
Likely secondary needs	
If Dominant	Power/Status/Money
If Detached	Rationality/Autonomy/Self-improvement
If Dependent	Acceptance/Approval
Public persona *If Dominant*	Winner
If Detached	Achiever
If Dependent	Catalyst
Self-image *If Winner*	Achiever
If Loser	Imposter
Prime parental injunction	Do your best/Be the best
Reinforced behavior	Winning
Acquired behavior	Competition
Heroes	Sports heroes; quantifiable achievers
Criteria of success	Winning
Conversation	Cites specific achievements, prizes
Psychic contract	To go on winning
Culminating achievement	Outstanding achievement
Underlying fear	Failure; being seen to be a loser
Likely emotional problem	Perfectionism; Overaggressiveness
House(s)	
Car(s)	
Significant other(s)	
Likely possessions	Trophies, prizes
Home furnishings	Trophies, prizes, photos of self competing, winning
Preferred pet(s)	Racehorse; show dog
Overall finances	
Readings: coffee table	
bedside	
School and college history	Active in competitive sports
Favorite subjects	Business, mathematics

WORK BEHAVIORS

Industry to which attracted	
Likely job function	Prefers role where can show consistent improvement

How came to apply for job	Referral from recruiter
Reason for applying	Greater challenge
Most enjoyed features	Opportunity to compete, excell
Least enjoyed features	Routine
Reason for leaving	Seeking greater challenge
Greatest contribution	Cites specific achievement related to profits or growth
Income pattern	Well paid; will take fixed income for opportunity to excel

PRIME NEED

POWER

Likely overall style		Dominant or Dominant/Dependent
Likely secondary needs		
	If Dominant	Status/Autonomy/Money
	If Dependent	Acceptance/Approval
	If Detached	Rationality/Autonomy/Achievement
Public persona	*If Dominant*	Leader
	If Detached	Manager
	If Dependent	Tough leader
Self-image	*If Winner*	Achiever
	If Loser	Helpless child
Prime parental injunction		Take charge
Reinforced behavior		Dominating
Acquired behavior		Social dominance
Heroes		Political leaders; Charles deGaulle, Margaret Thatcher
Criteria of success		Number of people managed
Conversation		Cites number of subordinates
Psychic contract		To rise in management ranks
Culminating achievement		CEO in medium/large company
Underlying fear(s)		Helplessness
Likely emotional problem		Overaggressiveness
House(s)		
Car(s)		Jaguar, Mercedes, Range Rover
Significant other(s)		
Likely possessions		
Home furnishings		Photos of self with politicians, business leaders
Preferred pet(s)		Alsatian dog
Overall finances		

Readings: coffee table	*Fortune* magazine
bedside	*Leaders,* by Richard Nixon; *Macbeth,* by William Shakespeare
School and college history	Active in student politics
Favorite subjects	Political science, history

WORK BEHAVIORS

Industry to which attracted	
Likely job function	Line management
How came to apply for job	Referral from powerful ally
Reason for applying	Seeks role where may dominate, direct, manipulate
Most enjoyed features	Managing others
Least enjoyed features	Lack of control
Reason for leaving	Seeking large management role
Greatest contribution	Cites number of people managed
Income pattern	Will forgo income for power; well paid if an effective manager and leader

PRIME NEED   RATIONALITY

Likely overall style		Detached
Likely secondary needs		
	If Detached	Autonomy/Achievement
	If Dominant	Autonomy/Achievement/Power
	If Dependent	Approval/Acceptance
Public persona	*If Detached*	Rational
	If Dependent	Rational and non-threatening
	If Dominant	Rational and achievement-oriented
Self-image	*If Winner*	Rational
	If Loser	Misunderstood
Prime parental injunction		Do your own thing; don't create conflict
Reinforced behavior		Rationality
Acquired behavior		Mediating
Heroes		Rational achievers, scientists
Criteria of success		Quantifiable achievement
Conversation		Specifies issues, defines terms

Psychic contract	To do own thing
Culminating achievement	Rational achievement, perhaps strategic turnaround
Underlying fear(s)	Will lose out because rationality fails to apply
Likely emotional problems	Perfectionism
House(s)	Functional
Car(s)	Functional, fuel-efficient
Significant other(s)	
Likely possessions	Personal computer; chess set
Home furnishings	Functional
Preferred pet(s)	None
Overall finances	Balanced; safe
Readings: coffee table	*Scientific American*
bedside	*Harvard Business Review*
School and college history	Strong student; cerebral extracurricular pursuits
Favorite subjects	Hard sciences, languages

WORK BEHAVIORS

Industry to which attracted	Hi-tech, computers, telecommunications
Likely job function	Strategic planning, marketing
How came to apply for job	Own careful job search
Reason for applying	Seeks role where may use planning and managerial skills to effect genuine accomplishment
Most enjoyed features	Problem solving
Least enjoyed features	Fuzzy elements
Reason for leaving	Seeking greater challenge
Greatest contribution	Cites specific quantifiable accomplishments
Income pattern	Consistent upward pattern

PRIME NEED   AFFILIATION

Likely overall style	Dependent
Likely secondary needs	
If Dependent	Acceptance/Approval
If Dominant	Acceptance/Status/Power
If Detached	Approval/Rationality/Achievement

Public persona	*If Dependent*	Non-threatening, nice
	If Dominant	Tough leader
	If Detached	Reliable, rational
Self-image	*If Winner*	Nice guy/gal
	If Loser	Rejected
Prime parental injunction		Get on with everyone
Reinforced behavior		Gregariousness
Acquired behavior		Empathy
Heroes		People with many relationships
Criteria of success		Number of friends and colleagues
Conversation		Speaks warmly of most people
Psychic contract		To win affection
Culminating achievement		Surprise 50th birthday party organized by friends
Underlying fear(s)		Rejection
Likely emotional problem		Lack of discipline
House(s)		Comfortable, homey
Car(s)		Run-of-the-mill station wagon
Significant other(s)		Dominating
Likely possessions		
Home furnishings		Photos of friends, family
Preferred pet(s)		Labrador dog
Overall finances		
Readings: coffee table		*People magazine*
bedside		*How to Win Friends and Influence People,* by Dale Carnegie
School and college history		Active in clubs, fraternities
Favorite subjects		Social sciences

WORK BEHAVIORS

Industry to which attracted	People industries, personnel, sales, travel, etc.
Likely job function	Advocacy/nurturing
How came to apply for job	Referral of friend, colleague
Reason for applying	Seeks role where may establish and enjoy relationships
Most enjoyed features	Relationships
Least enjoyed features	Working alone
Reason for leaving	Seeking greater opportunity to mix with others

Greatest contribution		Cites number and quality of friends, colleagues
Income pattern		May forgo income for people role

PRIME NEED

AUTONOMY

Likely overall style		Detached, or Dominant/Detached
Likely secondary needs		
	If Detached	Rationality/Achievement/Self-Improvement
	If Dominant	Achievement/Power/Rationality
	If Dependent	Status.
Public persona	*If Dominant*	Self-reliant, rational
	If Detached	Self-reliant, rational
	If Dependent	Strong, tough, feisty
Self-image	*If Winner*	Self-made
	If Loser	Dependent upon others
Prime parental injunction		Don't rely on others
Acquired behavior		Self-reliance
Heroes		Small successful entrepreneurs
Criteria of success		Financial independence
Conversation		Cites autonomy needs
Psychic contract		Attain financial independence
Culminating achievement		Establish own viable business
Underlying fear(s)		Fear of losing control
Likely emotional problem		Selfishness, rigidity
House(s)		
Car(s)		
Significant other(s)		Passive, submissive
Likely possessions		
Home furnishings		Portraits of self
Preferred pet(s)		
Overall finances		Fairly sound
Readings: coffee table		*Inc.* magazine
bedside		*How to Take Charge of Your Life,* by Mildred Newman and Bernard Berkowitz
School and college history		Loner; paid own way
Favorite subjects		Business

WORK BEHAVIORS

Industry to which attracted	Self-employment or opportunities to work without supervision
Likely job function	
How came to apply for job	Initiated own contact
Reason for applying	Seeks role where can work with minimum supervision
Most enjoyed features	Autonomy
Least enjoyed features	Lack of control, reporting to others
Reason for leaving	Greater autonomy
Greatest contribution	Emphasizes own rather than group accomplishments
Income pattern	Will forgo income for autonomy

PRIME NEED

SERVICE

Likely overall style		Dependent
Likely secondary needs		
	If Dependent	Acceptance/Approval
	If Dominant	Achievement/Power
	If Detached	Approval/Rationality/Achievement
Public persona	*If Dependent*	Non-threatening
	If Dominant	Achievement-oriented
	If Detached	Reliable, rational
Self-image	*If Winner*	Someone who made a difference
	If Loser	Let people down
Prime parental injunction		Do good for others
Reinforced behavior		Service
Acquired behavior		Helpfulness
Heroes		People in nurturing professions; Mother Teresa
Criteria of success		Number of people helped
Conversation		Shows concern for others
Psychic contract		To serve and help others
Culminating achievement		Awarded medal while chief of service organization
Underlying fear(s)		Rejection
Likely emotional problem		Emotional burnout; lack of realism
House(s)		Comfortable, homey
Car(s)		Run-of-the-mill station wagon

Significant other(s)	Dominating
Likely possessions	
Home furnishings	Photos of foster children
Preferred pet(s)	Labrador dog
Overall finances	Frugal
Readings: coffee table	
bedside	*How to Win Friends and Influence People,* by Dale Carnegie
School and college history	Active in service clubs
Favorite subjects	Social sciences

WORK BEHAVIORS

Industry to which attracted	Service
Likely job function	Nurturing
How came to apply for job	Referral from clergy or similar
Reason for applying	Seeks role where may help others
Most enjoyed features	Helping others
Least enjoyed features	Working alone, or solely for profit
Reason for leaving	Seeking greater opportunity to help others
Greatest contribution	Cites people helped
Income pattern	Will forgo income in order to serve

PRIME NEED

SECURITY

Likely overall style		Dependent or Detached
Likely secondary needs		
	If Dependent	Approval/Acceptance
	If Detached	Rationality/Achievement
	If Dominant	Power/Status
Public persona	*If Dependent*	
	If Dominant	
	If Detached	
Self-image	*If Winner*	
	If Loser	
Prime parental injunction		Be prudent, careful
Acquired behavior		Frugality
Heroes		People who own freehold homes
Criteria of success		Economic security

Conversation	Asks about insurance, pensions
Psychic contract	Establish economic security
Culminating achievement	Paying off mortgage
Underlying fear(s)	Fear of poverty
Likely emotional problem	Passivity
House(s)	Small to medium, tidy, in middle-class suburb
Car(s)	Fuel-efficient
Significant other(s)	
Likely possessions	
Home furnishings	Portrait of father or national leader
Preferred pet(s)	May breed pets for sale
Overall finances	Prudent, sound
Readings: coffee table	
bedside	*Wealth Without Risk*
School and college history	
Favorite subjects	

WORK BEHAVIORS

Industry to which attracted	Large, established, secure
Likely job function	Middle management
How came to apply for job	Outplacement program
Reason for applying	Seeks secure role, probably not in sales
Most enjoyed features	Security
Least enjoyed features	Lack of security
Reason for leaving	Greater security
Greatest contribution	Cost savings
Income pattern	Will forgo income for security

PRIME NEED

STATUS

Likely overall style		Dominant or Dependent
Likely secondary needs		
	If Dominant	Power/Status
	If Dependent	Acceptance/Approval
	If Detached	Autonomy/Achievement
Public persona	If Dominant	Powerful leader
	If Dependent	Highly successful salesperson
	If Detached	Unlikely, but probably achievement, rationality
Self-image	If Winner	Impostor
	If Loser	Social outcast

Prime parental injunction	Maintain reputation and appearances
Acquired behavior	Conspicuous display of status
Heroes	Old-moneyed relations
Criteria of success	Conspicuous status
Conversation	Name and address dropper
Psychic contract	Furtherance of social pretensions
Culminating achievement	Name in *Social Register*
Underlying fear(s)	Gnawing sense of inferiority
Likely emotional problem	Wishful thinker
House(s)	Smallest in well-to-do suburb, or largest in otherwise down-at-heel area
Car(s)	Two leased European cars
Significant other(s)	Status object
Likely possessions	
Home furnishings	Original art
Preferred pet(s)	Siamese cat
Overall finances	Shaky, strained
Readings: coffee table	*Social Register*
bedside	*Architectural Digest*
School and college history	Ordinary record at elite private institutions
Favorite subjects	Art history

WORK BEHAVIORS

Industry to which attracted	Glamor or blue chip
Likely job function	Sales or public relations
How came to apply for job	Well-placed contact or outplacement program
Reason for applying	Seeks high-visibility sales or advisory role
Most enjoyed features	Visibility, contacts
Least enjoyed features	Lack of status
Reason for leaving	Being squeezed out
Greatest contribution	Improve company's image, promoting own visibility
Income pattern	Money-hungry but forgoes income for status

PRIME NEED	MONEY
	for its own sake, not merely to ease security or short-term needs.
Likely overall style	Dominant/Dependent
Likely secondary needs	
If Dominant	Status/Autonomy/Power
If Dependent	Status/Acceptance
If Detached	Status/Achievement/Autonomy
Public persona *If Dominant*	Successful, financially comfortable
If Dependent	Successful, financially comfortable
If Detached	Achiever
Self-image *If Winner*	Holding finances together
If Loser	Impostor
Prime parental injunction	Study hard
Acquired behavior	Big spending
Heroes	Rich celebrities
Criteria of success	$$$ and status
Conversation	Real estate prices; published lists of top earners
Psychic contract	To become financial success— or failure
Culminating achievement	Forbes list of richest people; purchase of yacht or Lear jet
Underlying fear(s)	Poverty and rejection
Likely emotional problem	Narcissistic, wishful thinker
House(s)	Big, status-filled
Car(s)	Expensive European; leased
Significant other(s)	Trophy
Likely possessions	Second home; motor cruiser American Express Platinum Card; well-used credit lines
Home furnishings	Original art, "name" artists
Preferred pet(s)	Trophy friends
Overall finances	Stretched
Readings: coffee table	*Architectural Digest*
bedside	*Forbes* magazine
School and college history	Very average record at ordinary schools
Favorite subjects	Soft subjects and business

WORK BEHAVIORS

Industry to which attracted	Entrepreneurial
Likely job function	Sales or marketing
How came to apply for job	Contact upon hearing of money-earning opportunities
Reason for applying	More money
Most enjoyed features	Dealmaking for commissions
Least enjoyed features	Activity unrelated to income
Reason for leaving	Seeking more money
Greatest contribution	Income earned
Income pattern	Forgoes fixed salary for share of profits, commissions

PRIME NEED

INVESTIGATE

Likely overall style		Detached
Likely secondary needs		
	If Detached	Achievement/Autonomy
	If Dependent	Service/Approval
	If Dominant	Autonomy/Achievement/Self-Improvement
Public persona	If Detached	Nonconformist
	If Dominant	Rational achiever
	If Dependent	Dreamer
Self-image	If Winner	Creative
	If Loser	Creative
Prime parental injunction		Study hard
Acquired behavior		Curiosity, analysis
Heroes		Scientists, inventors
Criteria of success		Creativity, problem solving
Conversation		Scientific issues; pursuit of "truth"; cites own published articles
Psychic contract		To do own thing
Culminating achievement		Patented invention
Underlying fear(s)		Lack of time or resources to pursue interests
Likely emotional problem		Unrealistic dreamer
House(s)		Nothing special
Car(s)		Small, functional
Significant other(s)		
Likely possessions		Personal computer; serious camera

Home furnishings	Functional
Preferred pet(s)	White rats
Overall finances	Modest
Readings: coffee table	*National Geographic*
bedside	*Scientific American*
School and college history	Good record in hard sciences and research; not much interest in social pursuits
Favorite subjects	Hard sciences

WORK BEHAVIORS

Industry to which attracted	Hi-tech, pharmaceuticals, chemical, computer
Likely job function	Research officer
How came to apply for job	Initiated own approach upon hearing of research opportunity
Reason for applying	Creative challenge
Most enjoyed features	Research, creative challenge
Least enjoyed features	Company housekeeping
Reason for leaving	Seeking greater creative challenge elsewhere
Greatest contribution	Specific invention or technique
Income pattern	Forgoes money, power for creative opportunities

INDICES OF EMOTIONAL IMMATURITY

The most effective way to spot maturity is to identify indices of *im*maturity in a person's behavior, manner, and conversation.

EMOTIONAL OVERDEPENDENCY

Seeks an organization to support him/her rather than somewhere to work

Overconcern with pensions, seniority, security

Prefers soft job with few demands

Needs structured role

Prefers routine tasks

Doesn't like to make decisions
Lengthy stints of unemployment
No strong effort to become employed
Depends on others to locate jobs
Failed to contribute to cost of education
Failed to graduate for "lack of finances"
Overconcern with health and well-being

SELFISHNESS

Job history indicates self-centeredness or disloyalty
Will not go the extra mile unless paid to do so
A loner
Manipulative; uses people
Overly concerned with status roles and symbols
Boastful
A credit grabber
A blamer
A conversation monopolizer

PLEASURE-MINDEDNESS

Childlike natural charm
Good fun to be with, playful
Pleasure-before-business attitude
Erratic or short-term employment
Takes "sick" days
Goes on ill-timed vacations
Won't work at what he/she doesn't like
Postpones unpleasant work
Seeks work with highly flexible hours
Stints of non-employment to pursue pleasure interests
Took soft subjects at school and college
Did not make the effort to graduate
School activities primarily recreational

WISHFUL THINKING

Unrealistic job and salary expectations
Overestimates ability to take advancement
Inflates importance of previous jobs, earnings, numbers of
people supervised
Indications of poor judgment in previous jobs
Daydreams about success, but does not pursue it

Studied for glamor fields beyond his/her capabilities at school

Asserts can achieve "magic" by thinking positively

Overextended financially

UNWILLINGNESS TO ACCEPT RESPONSIBILITY

Blames others for personal failures and shortcomings

Quits job with nowhere to go

Coasts between jobs

Lets others support him/her

Nine to fiver

General unwillingness to pay own way

No interest in maintaining or developing a career

Little or no interest in self-improvement

Lives at home till well into twenties

INCAPACITY FOR SELF-DISCIPLINE

Easily upset

Quick-tempered

Can't take criticism

Stints of unemployment following angry walkouts

Temper tantrums leading to accidents

School or college dropout

Failed to apply self at school

Overprotected or indulged childhood

Constant relationship problems

Broken relationships

Shaky finances stemming from impulsive purchases

Drug, alcohol, or nicotine abuse

DISREGARD FOR CONSEQUENCES

Erratic job history

Quits job with nowhere to go

Impulsive vacationer

Inappropriate, irresponsible, or insensitive comments during interview

Quits school or college on whim

Quits relationships on impulse

Lives beyond means

History of shaky finances

OVERCONFORMISM

Conservative upbringing
Pious
Fundamentalist religion
Rigid dress standards
Attracted to large, secure companies
Bureaucratic job roles
Finances very conservative
Rigidly punctual
Fiercely conservative political outlook
Hesitant to advance an authentic opinion
Overly respectful of all forms of authority

SHOWOFF TENDENCIES

Lives to a high style or status
Overvalues symbols of status
Attracted to limelight work roles
Seeks center of attention in private life
Difficulty differentiating notoriety from reputation
Publicity seeker
Compulsive joker
Attention-getting clothes; sartorial splendor
Active in debating, drama, during schooling
Life of the party
Excessive pride in flashy possessions
Dominates conversation
Uses ill health to attract attention

DESTRUCTIVE TENDENCIES

Constant complainer
Unnecessarily rebellious
Overly critical of others
Criticizes previous employers
Criticizes colleges, teachers
Evidence of dangerous driving
Motor vehicle accidents
Chronic financial problems
Prior bankrupt
Alcohol or nicotine abuser

WORK HABITS: OVERVIEW

OVERALL POSITIVE OMENS

Energy level	High
Prime need	Achievement
Key injunctions and example	Work hard, excell, persevere. Have fun, live a balanced, happy life. Don't strive unnecessarily
Reinforced behavior	Industry, perseverance, self-reliance
Acquired behavior	Contributed to family finances; left home early to make own way
Heroes	Hard workers
Conversation	Cites hardworking parents, personal obstacles overcome
House(s)	Tidy, well maintained, containing den, workroom
Significant other(s)	Hardworking progeny of hardworking parents
Résumé	Personal letter. Cites high grade-point averages and work-oriented achievements; cites employment month by month; mentions sporting interests and accomplishments

OVERALL NEGATIVE OMENS

Energy level	*Low*
Prime need	Status
Key injunctions and example	*Have fun, live a balanced, happy life. Don't strive unnecessarily*
Reinforced behavior	Conformism, indolence, dependence; slowness to leave family womb
Acquired behavior	Lack of initiative, laziness, dependence
Heroes	Father figures, celebrities, film stars
Conversation	Cites need to balance work and pleasure
House(s)	Untidy, poorly maintained

Significant other(s)	Pleasure-oriented
School and college history	Failed to make financial contribution; pursued soft courses; dropped out, or failed to complete on time
Résumé	Prepared by outplacement firm. Fails to cite key dates, omits months, lists clubs; preoccupation with titles

KEY BEHAVIORAL TRAITS

INDUSTRY

KEY QUESTIONS

- Is this person driven by the voice of conscience?
- Is he/she pulled along by achievement needs?
- Is the habit of industry ingrained?

How came to apply for job	Own initiative *Referral from previous superior*
Reason for applying	Shows good understanding of demands of the job. Does not appear to be seeking an easy job. Has done some homework *Ill prepared. Apparently seeking soft role*
Most enjoyed features	Enjoyed most aspects of the work. Not picky *Very picky. Likes easy work*
Least enjoyed features	Spells without enough work *Too much work. "Workaholic" boss. Too much pressure*
Hours worked	Works in excess of forty to fifty hours a week. Regards overtime as an opportunity to get ahead *Aversive to overtime. Seldom works more than forty-hour week*
Work history	Steady progress and promotion. Regular merit awards *"Overlooked" by superiors. Not much promotion*

Greatest contribution	Cites specific, quantifiable, on-the-job achievements *Cites improvement in morale or similar fuzzy items*
Reason for leaving	Seeking greater challenge *Overlooked. Too much pressure. Too many demands*
Income pattern	Pattern of increasing income. Receives an above-average income for the industry *Little or very modest automatic increase in income. Average or below-average earner*
Family background	Began working early in life. Contributed to family finances. Constructive spare-time interests. Always busy *Indulged, pleasure seeker*
School and college history	Made financial contribution. Ran on-campus business. Achievements in line with abilities *Very modest achievements. Vacationed with parents in Europe*
Favorite subjects	Pursued difficult subjects *Pursued soft options*
Domestic and social	Chooses constructive hobbies and interests, and becomes proficient in them. Steady in relationships, works at them if necessary. *Pattern of broken relationships. Hedonistic part-time interests*
Finances	Persistently builds up net worth. Works hard to repay necessary loans *Shaky finances*

PERSEVERANCE

KEY QUESTIONS

- Is this person driven to complete what he/she begins?
- Is the habit of perseverance ingrained?

How came to apply for job	Own initiative
Reason for applying	Seeking new challenge for sound reason *Simply quitting last job*
Most enjoyed features	Overcoming obstacles, solving problems *Routine, structured activity*
Least enjoyed features	Unchallenging work *Too many obstacles. Job just "impossible"*
Hours worked	"Will do whatever it takes to complete the job" *Regular nine to fiver, come what may*
Work history	Stays with tough assignments and completes them. Persists in the face of difficulty. Keeps going *Quits when going gets rough. Gives up easily*
Greatest contribution	Cites specific, quantifiable, on-the-job achievements *Cites improvement in morale or similar fuzzy items*
Reason for leaving	Challenge completed, and seeking new fields to conquer *"Insurmountable problems in present role"*
Income pattern	Pattern of increasing income. Receives an above-average income for the industry. Will take pay cut to ride out a recession, however *Little or very modest automatic increase in income. Marginally average earner*
Family background	Parents valued perseverance. Stressed need to complete education. Has overcome disadvantaged upbringing
School and college history	Completed whatever took on. Won scholarships and special awards. Completed despite financial difficulties. Completed

	night or correspondence classes *Dropout or maybe college switch in midstream*
Domestic and social	Shows unusual proficiency in hobbies and interests *Pattern of broken relationships. Varied, fleeting part-time interests*
Finances	Persistently builds up net worth
Health	Has worked to overcome a physical health problem, or has used same as spur to achievement *Worries that health may suffer if works too hard. Uses poor health as excuse for laziness*

SELF-RELIANCE

KEY QUESTIONS

- Did this person learn to be self-reliant as a child?
- Is the habit of self-reliance ingrained?

How came to apply for job	Pursuing definite goals. Sounds confident of abilities *Contact arranged by friend*
Reason for applying	Furtherance of career *Primarily seeking secure employment*
Most enjoyed features	Opportunity to exercise independence of mind, make decisions, assume responsibility *Routine, structured activity*
Least enjoyed features	Routine, structured activity *Operating in ambiguous situations*
Work history	Pattern of taking increased responsibility in decision-making roles, with little or no supervision. Initiates and implements new projects *Leans on superiors, goes by company manual. A follower*
Greatest contribution	Was initiator or key operator of this project

Reason for leaving

Follower in someone else's plan or achievement

Shows initiative in seeking new role. Depends on own finances or efforts during any unemployment

Subsists on finances or efforts of others

Family background

Parents instilled self-reliance. Contributed to own or family finances. Showed initiative in hobbies, sports. Upward mobility despite social disadvantages. Left home early

Developed feeling of entitlement. All or most needs taken care of by indulgent parents. Slow to leave family home

School and college history

Contributed to finances. Chose own colleges and courses. Officer in school activities

Mostly a passive participant. Rationalizes non-attendance through poor family finances

Domestic and social

Shows initiative in pursuing interests and hobbies. Leadership roles in community or social affairs. Dominant or equal partner in relationship with s/o

Finances

Finances sound. Could withstand rainy day without help from others

Dependent upon income of s/o or family members

Health

Assumes responsibility for own health and fitness. Gets regular exercise

Dependent upon alcohol, nicotine to control moods. Overdependent upon doctors and medications

PEOPLE SKILLS

PEERS—AND GENERAL

KEY QUESTIONS

- Does the subject possess a realistic appreciation of the need to get along with people on the job?
- Is the subject empathetic: do I enjoy his/her company and want to prolong the conversation?
- Do the answers show tact?
- Are there any signs of hostility or latent hostility?
- Does he/she needlessly criticize others?
- Would I be happy to deal with him/her on a regular basis?
- If the subject shows great charm, might this mask underlying immaturity and a wish to misdirect attention from his/her actual track record?
- Has the subject established good relationships with all the key people in his/her life?

How came to apply for job	Welcomes opportunity to meet and mix with new people
Most enjoyed features	Enjoys mixing with others *Prefers working alone*
Least enjoyed features	Periods of isolation *"Having to work with difficult people"*
Work history	Appreciates the need to get along with people, on the job, and makes the effort to do so. Pattern of getting along with most people. Speaks well of former peers and associates *Criticizes former peers, expresses doubts about their ethics or personal standards*
Reason for leaving	*Terminated for no apparent reason, or on basis of being disliked, or "personality clash"*
Family background	Good relationships with siblings. Learned early to cooperate with others

School and college history	Got along with other kids. Enjoyed group activities. Elected officer in social roles
Domestic and social	Engages in social activities where has to mix as an equal with others. Good relationships with s/o's. Entertains friends at home
	Avoids social situations. Poor relationships with s/o's. Enjoys racist or sexist jokes
Health	Shows empathy toward others' health problems
	Evidences Shadenfreude (vindictive pleasure) in misfortunes of others

SUPERIORS

KEY QUESTIONS

- Does the subject display loyalty to past employers, enjoy good relationships with them, identify with them? Was the subject pleased to be "on the team"?
- Is there evidence of an underlying antipathy toward authority: criticism of the government, the police, past bosses or schoolteachers, spouse, in-laws, or parents?

How came to apply for job	Referral from past superior
	Personality clash with present superior
Most enjoyed features	Interaction with superiors
	Working "without intrusion"
Least enjoyed features	*Unnecessary intrusion from boss*
Work history	Appreciates the need for intelligent direction. Pattern of getting on with past superiors. Does not expect boss to be perfect. Enjoys respect of past superiors
	Adversarial attitude to former superiors. Doubts their ethics, competence, intelligence, intentions
Reason for leaving	*Terminated for no apparent reason, or on basis of being disliked, or "personality clash"*

Family background	Good relationship with father or key disciplinary figure *Shaky relationship with either parent or key disciplinary figure. Latchkey child, or black sheep*
School and college history	Got along with teachers. Did not run into problems with "the system" *Problems with teachers. Expelled or suspended*
Domestic and social	Comfortable mixing socially with superiors, or older people of higher status

SUBORDINATES

KEY QUESTIONS

- Does the subject's history reveal any pattern of election to leadership roles?
- Does the subject inspire the kind of confidence, admiration, and trust that would inspire others to seek his/her help and guidance?

How came to apply for job	Referral from former subordinate or peer. Displays presence and realistic confidence
Most enjoyed features	Managing others, resolving conflict, getting people motivated *Working alone*
Least enjoyed features	*"Managing difficult people"*
Work history	Talks of goals, strategies, and results "we" accomplished. Consistently promoted into increasingly responsible managerial roles. Appreciates overall need to balance results and morale. Expects to have to win respect, and shows confidence to do so. Enjoys the job of managing more than the title of manager *Overlooked for managerial role, or demoted from one. Cites need for tough or aggressive management.*

Reason for leaving

Boosts self as strong leader and talks in terms of results "I" accomplished
More challenging managerial role following successful turn-around, or similar
Company reneged on promise to promote into management. Lack of managerial prospects. Division formerly lead by subject failed due to "poor market," lack or morale, or similar alibi

Family background

Developed habit of leadership at an early age. Indications of leadership ability in childhood spare-time interests

School and college history

Elected to leadership roles at school. Performed successfully in such roles

Domestic and social

Dominant person in the home. Holds authentic leadership roles in community affairs

CLIENTS

KEY QUESTIONS

- Is the subject empathetic? Do I (and would a client) enjoy his/her company and want to prolong the conversation?
- Can the subject strike an appropriate balance between aggression and empathy? Will he/she want to sell the client—or just make conversation?

How came to apply for job

Own initiative. Welcomes opportunity to sell self, tactfully

Most enjoyed features

Enjoyed making sales, and measures success in actual sales results

Work history

Appreciates the need to prospect for and bring in new business. Successful sales record. Has built up a clientele
Aversive to developing leads. Inferior sales record. No current personal following or clientele

Family background

Manipulative and persuasive abilities instilled

School and college history	Sales and advocacy roles. Active in debating or drama. Competitive. Took sales or entrepreneurial role to pay for education
Domestic and social	Gregarious. Many friends. Keen to establish new relationships. Well liked by old friends

BASIC ENERGY LEVEL

How came to apply for job	Looking for job requiring energy and drive *Prefers undemanding role*
Most enjoyed features	Enjoys pressure situations and demanding, challenging work
Least enjoyed features	Slower-paced, physically unchallenging work
Work history	Attracted to roles requiring intense or prolonged physical or mental effort. Seeks variety, complexity, and tempo. Any underlying anxieties spur great effort and accomplishment. May have held more than one job at a time *Nine to fiver. Prefers routine roles*
Greatest contribution	Required high energy level *Subsists on finances or efforts of others*
Family background	Energetic parents and siblings. Active in physical pursuits as a child *Sickly or low-energy parents or siblings.* Passive interests as a child
School and college history	Paid own way. Completed on time or earlier. Active in demanding physical pursuits. Wide range of active interests
Domestic and social	Active in many activities, including physical sports and activities
Health	No health problems. *Health problems—and absenteeism—reflect physical deterioration*

If you would like to receive information on Wareham corporate services or publications please write to:

John Wareham
Wareham Associates, Inc.
Senior Human Resource Consultants
152 East 63rd Street
New York, NY 10021.